WALT WHITMAN'S NEW YORK

WALT

FROM MANHATTAN

WHITMAN'S

TO MONTAUK

NEW YORK

Edited by Henry M. Christman

BOOKS FOR LIBRARIES PRESS

FREEPORT, NEW YORK

Library of Congress Cataloging in Publication Data

Whitman, Walt, 1819-1892.
    Walt Whitman's New York.

    ([BCL/select bibliographies reprint series])
    "On June 8, 1861, the Brooklyn standard published
the first of an unsigned series of [the author's] ...
articles to which the newspaper gave the title of
'Brooklyniana.' It is these articles that appear in
this book."
    1. New York (City)--History--Addresses, essays,
lectures. 2. Brooklyn--History--Addresses, essays,
lectures. 3. Long Island--History, Local--Addresses,
essays, lectures. I. Title.
F128.3.W5 1972   974.71'03   74-39704
ISBN 0-8369-9933-9

F
128.3
·W5
1972

PRINTED IN THE UNITED STATES OF AMERICA
BY
NEW WORLD BOOK MANUFACTURING CO., INC
HALLANDALE, FLORIDA 33009

MANNAHATTA

My city's fit and noble name resumed,
Choice aboriginal name, with marvellous beauty, meaning,
A rocky founded island—shores where ever gayly dash the
  coming, going, hurrying sea waves.

—Walt Whitman, from *Leaves of Grass*

PAUMANOK

SEA-BEAUTY! stretch'd and basking!
One side thy inland ocean laving, broad, with copious
  commerce, steamers, sails,
And one the Atlantic's wind caressing, fierce or gentle-
  mighty hulls dark-gliding in the distance.
Isle of sweet brooks of drinking-water—healthy air and
  soil!
Isle of the salty shore and breeze and brine!

—Walt Whitman, from *Leaves of Grass*

INTRODUCTION

The work that follows constitutes a remarkable Whitman manuscript, one that up to now has been accessible only to the specialist. It originally appeared in the form of newspaper articles, and therefore is journalism. But it is also historiography, for which Whitman compiled material from written sources and from interviews. Finally, the work contains a considerable amount of Whitman autobiography—reminiscences from Whitman's childhood and experiences from his youth. Accounts from Colonial and Revolutionary records, memories related by longtime residents, and Whitman's own reactions and experiences all blend together into an unusual work that bears the unmistakable imprint of Whitman's personality.

Whitman's life is so well known that it hardly needs to be reviewed at length. However, it might well be useful for the reader to have in mind the basic periods of Whitman's career, so that this work can be placed in proper chronological perspective.

Walt Whitman was born on May 31, 1819, in the farming community of West Hills, Long Island, in western Suffolk County. At the age of three, Whitman was moved to Brooklyn with his family, and it was there that he spent his childhood. While still in his teens, Whitman left the family home in Brooklyn, and spent some five years at several occupations at various locations on Long Island. He served as a schoolteacher, and as writer, editor, and printer for newspapers. During this period he lived and worked in what are now the urban and suburban counties of Queens, Nassau, and Suffolk. At that time, however, this area was rural, with only small scattered villages.

While in his early twenties, Whitman returned to the city, living and working in both Manhattan and Brooklyn as writer, editor, and printer for various newspapers. This was to be his life for the next twenty years until the Civil

War brought about his move to Washington, D.C. Probably his most famous post during this period was his tenure as editor of the Brooklyn *Eagle*.

By the summer of 1855, Whitman had published the first edition of *Leaves of Grass*. A second edition appeared the following year, and, in 1860, a third edition. Whitman was forty-two years old and something of a local personage when, on June 8, 1861, the Brooklyn *Standard* published the first of an unsigned series of his articles to which the newspaper gave the title of "Brooklyniana." It is these articles that appear in this book.

Of all Whitman's New York journalism this "Brooklyniana" series is of greatest interest. Since this series was prepared as a unit it has a continuity not found in Whitman's other journalism. Nor was he working against the usual newspaper deadline. Indeed there is reason to believe that Whitman originally intended to write a somewhat longer manuscript and publish it, not as journalism, but in book form, and then decided later to release it for newspaper publication. In any event, this continuation of articles has the type of organization, research, and continuity seldom found in the journalism of the day.

The series is organized on a geographic basis. The first sections deal with Manhattan and Brooklyn, while in the later pieces Whitman moves eastward across Long Island.

It is of interest, and useful, to review very briefly some of the major changes in geographical and governmental entities that have taken place since Whitman wrote this work. New York City then included only what are today the Borough of Manhattan and part of the Borough of the Bronx; and, in practice, when these articles were written, "New York City" or "Manhattan" meant lower Manhattan. Manhattan north of Forty-second Street was largely rural. When Whitman wrote these articles, Brooklyn was an independent city, consisting of what are today the Brooklyn Heights, downtown Brooklyn, South Brooklyn, and Williamsburg areas. Kings County—which today comprises New York City's Borough of Brooklyn—was mostly rural, and, in addition to Brooklyn, contained other, independent communities such as Flatbush and Gravesend. What is today New York City's Borough of Queens was also rural, with independent communities such as Jamaica and Flushing; and what is today suburban Nassau County did not even exist at that time; it was part of rural Queens County. Nassau County was formed later by splitting the original Queens County into two new counties.

As the reader will see, Whitman, though a native of the New York area, loved it and wrote of it with the zeal and zest usually found only in those from elsewhere who have made New York their chosen home. One of Whitman's favorite pastimes was to stroll through the streets of Manhattan and Brooklyn, observing people, and making new friends. He became an enthusiastic devotee of the opera. And he also enjoyed the natural beauty to be found in the meadows and on the beaches of rural Long Island. In these very articles, Whitman writes with deep affection of both the urban Manhattan-Brooklyn area and of rural Long Island, which he preferred to call by its original Indian name of "Paumanok."

Yet Whitman did not merely use the New York area for his own pleasure; he was active in civic life. Through his association with newspapers, he encouraged and participated in crusades for social and civic improvement. He fought municipal corruption, working to expose the graft that seemed to flourish continually in every municipal department and every municipal enterprise. He was in the forefront of those defending what has become New York City's collection of beautiful parks, helping to fight off the real-estate speculators of the day. And hospitals were a special interest of Whitman's; he made particular efforts to publicize the services and needs of worthy hospitals.

All these activities are, of course, generally of the conventional "good government" variety—but some of Whitman's other civic views were less conventional. He was a strong critic of the law-enforcement, judicial, and penal systems as they were applied against the outcasts of society such as the prostitutes. It appalled Whitman to see the prostitutes of the city abused by brutal police and sanctimonious politicians who themselves were notoriously corrupt. Whitman also was a sharp critic of the hypocrisy he found among the clergy of the city.

Political activity of his day centered upon three parties— the Democrats, the Republicans, and the "Know-Nothings," more formally referred to as the Native American Party. The Democratic Party was split into two factions. The "Old Hunkers" were conservative Democrats, strongly pro-business, and pro-slavery. They were opposed within the party by progressive Democrats who were anti-slavery and who advocated greater social and economic democracy. Whitman was an active member of this latter faction, even serving as an official delegate to various Democratic Party conventions and gatherings.

Indeed, Whitman was a very active citizen, serving his city in a variety of ways. And it should be kept in mind that when Whitman wrote this work—articles dealing with Manhattan, Brooklyn, and Long Island—he had spent his entire life in this region, excepting only a brief stay in New Orleans. Interestingly, his best journalism on the subject of New York regional history came just at the time that the approach of the Civil War already had begun to disrupt and transform the region and the entire nation. In regard to Whitman personally, it is perhaps ironic that, so soon after he sang the praises of the New York area in this work, he was destined to leave this region of his birth and youth.

Whitman went to the Washington, D.C., area in December of 1862 in search of a brother in the Union Army who had been reported as wounded in action. He found his brother, only slightly wounded, safe in one of the Union camps. Thereafter, Whitman turned to visiting the Washington hospitals, seeking out wounded soldiers from the New York area. Whitman was so affected by his experiences in Washington hospitals that he undertook volunteer, unpaid nursing service there. Remaining in Washington, Whitman accepted a clerkship in the Federal government, giving all his spare time to the hospitals and to his writing. He was to spend the next ten years in Washington, and his final twenty years in Camden, New Jersey, where he died on March 26, 1892, at the age of seventy-two.

Whitman's New York years not only constituted his formative period but also comprised the greater part of his life. The first forty-two of Whitman's seventy-two years were spent in the New York area. It was in this region that he formed his philosophy of life and art—in short, the ideas and the style that distinguish his writings. This work is tangible evidence of the deep affection with which Whitman regarded the New York area, and the significance he attached to its history and traditions.

In editing this book, I have taken care to present Whitman's work as he wished and intended it to be presented. Some of the articles were considerably longer than others; several of these were broken down into installments by the *Standard*. I have restored them as Whitman wrote them, with the original continuity. When the series was published in the *Standard*, it was marred by numerous typographical errors. Such typographical errors distract readers, and I saw no valid reason for perpetuating them; again, I restored Whitman's work as he wrote it. At the same time, I felt that the headlines which the *Standard* placed over the articles serve a useful purpose for the contemporary reader, as well as providing a further authentic touch of the period, and so I have retained them. And, of course, I have preserved Whitman's distinctive style; I have not attempted to "modernize" it, but instead have left it in its original form, even with occasionally archaic spelling and punctuation.

Here, then, are Walt Whitman's observations and reminiscences on Manhattan-Brooklyn-Long Island life and history, as he wrote them and intended them to appear.

HENRY M. CHRISTMAN

I

PRESERVING TRADITIONS

DUTCH FOUNDATION OF BROOKLYN

OURS THE REAL FIRST SETTLEMENTS

PAUMANOK

1671

NARCISSUS DE SILLÉ

MICHAEL HAINELLE

THE ENGLISH GOVERNORSHIP

THE FIRST DUTCH MINISTER

REBELLIOUS SPIRIT

A New York journal, a few days ago, made the remark in the course of one of its articles that the whole spirit of a floating and changing population like ours is antagonistic to the recording and preserving of what traditions we have of the American past. This is probably too true. Few think of the events and persons departed from the stage, now in the midst of the turmoil and excitement of the great play of life and business going on around us. Especially is this the case in the huge cities of our Atlantic seaboard, like Brooklyn and New York, filled with a comparatively fresh population, *not* descendants of the old residenters, and without hereditary interest in the locations and their surroundings. Of course, such traditionary interest is not to be expected in the great Far West, either, at present. The settlers there have to construct the foundations of their own and society's edifice, with due firmness and security, long before they can have leisure for such retrospections.

Still, there will come a time, here in Brooklyn, and all over America, when nothing will be of more interest than authentic reminiscences of the past. Much of it will be made up of subordinate "memoirs," and of personal chronicles and gossip—but we think every portion of it will always meet a welcome from the large mass of American readers.

The foundation of the personnel of the settlement of Brooklyn, as is well known, comes from the Holland Dutch. In some respects, this side of the river has more claims to be considered the representative first settlement of the Dutch in the New World than the location of our neighbors over westward of the East River. For the Island of Manhattan, when pitched upon by the first voyageurs from Amsterdam, was selected mainly as their outpost or place for a trading station, a store and fort—and not for residences. Their residence, even from the beginning, was *here*. Manhattan Island, sterile and sandy, on a foundation of rock, was not an inviting looking spot, but bleak, sterile, and rough. So the first employees of the great Amsterdam Trading Association (the Dutch West India Company) made their settlement here on the aboriginal Island of Paumanok (or *Paumanake,* as it is also sometimes spelt in the old Indian deeds). Here, on the west end of this said Paumanok Island, they found a beautifully rich country, sufficiently diversified with slopes and hills, well wooded, yet with open ground enough—to their eyes, indeed (used to the flats and dykes, and treeless tameness of their Belgic dominions), a superb paradise of a country. And here they settled.

We do not design to undertake, at present, a sketch of the early settlement of Brooklyn by the Dutch, although we purpose doing so in another of our papers—or in some other form—for it is in every way worthy of being preserved, for the use of future Brooklynites.

The official records of Brooklyn are to be traced back, in an unbroken line, as far as 1671—although we believe the existence of the township, as an organization, dates a number of years before that period. At that date, authority was wielded under the umbrage of a charter granted by the States General of Holland to the Amsterdam Trading Company (the Dutch West India Company), who deputed both civil and ecclesiastical power as to them seemed fit—yet always, with candor be it said, for the advantage and improvement of the common people, and not for the selfish interests of a few. In this respect they made a marked contrast with the action of the powers afterward, under the English royal charters, whose action seemed to be wielded with reference to the glory and profit of some minion of the court—and whatever franchises the people secured they got only by turbulent complaints, sullen anger, or hard fighting.

Under the Dutch charter, a town organization was early

effected, the principal officer being simply a "town clarke." In 1671, this position was held by Herr Narcissus de Sillé—who continued in place for several years afterwards. The subordinate trustees were, during the same period, two other worthy men, immigrants also from Holland, named Frederick Lubertse and Peter Pernideau.

In 1675 the direction of their primitive municipal affairs, by the settlers, was confided to Michael Hainelle, who seems to have given great satisfaction, for he was continued in office down to 1690—being only re-chosen every year.

During this period, however, the English held the governorship of the province, having taken it in 1664. It is true, in the war of 1672, commenced by the English Charles 2d against the Dutch, the latter had, for a short time, resumed possession of their own colony, taking it under a fleet of ships from Holland—but the English soon re-took it again—or rather it was returned to them in 1674. Sir Edmund Andros was then sent over from England as governor.

Still, the settlement of Brooklyn and Manhattan Island, to all intents and purposes, was essentially Dutch, not only in its social and religious, but in its political customs and institutions. Be it remembered, too, that the Dutch were ahead of all other races in their regard for moral and intellectual development. At the very earliest schools and churches were established.

In this connection, as there has been, among Brooklyn and New York antiquaries, something of a dispute as to when the first Hollandic clergyman was sent over, we may mention a discovery made by our Minister to the Hague, Henry C. Murphy, which sets this question at rest. It is proved that almost contemporary with the settlement of Brooklyn and New York, (1623–30) the thoughtful providers in the mother country, under the grant from the States General, thought it incumbent on them to send out a

"Dominie," almost in the first party of emigrants. The discovery we allude to is of an original letter, in the old Amsterdam archives, of which Mr. Murphy sends a translation, which we have seen. It proves, as we say, that there was an accredited minister sent out at the very commencement. The name of this minister was Johannes Michaelius, and this letter is written, "at Manhatas, in Nieu-Netherland," in the year 1628. It describes his coming out to this same Brooklyn of ours, his experience on the voyage, and the appearance and condition of the county and people here and at what is now in New York City. The letter is a very great curiosity, and undoubtedly authentic. It is addressed to Dominie Adrianus Smoutries, minister of the Dutch Reformed Church at Amsterdam. It was found among the papers of the late Jacobus Korning, Clerk of the Fourth Judicial District of Amsterdam, and comes to light through the researches of Mr. Nijenpias, an explorer of Dutch records. We think our readers will join us in the assumption that this letter, with the mould of over two hundred and thirty years upon it, and relating exclusively to the settlement of these parts by one of the most interesting races of the earth, is a relic of profound sanctity to all Brooklynites, and that we ought to have it verbatim.

The schoolmaster was also provided for from the beginning. A school was required to be kept up in the settlement, and provision made for the support of the teacher. We have data of such old Dutch schools, here in Brooklyn, and at Flatbush, very far back. The original Dutch, it ought to be known, were among the most learned nations of Europe. The universities of Holland were among the best. Libraries were well stocked—and the invention of printing was really discovered there.

As an evidence of the sturdy spirit of those ancient days, existing in Brooklyn, we find the following old record, relating to 1698. At this time the English governor, Schuyler, was not very popular among the people; and there was a war (simply a king's quarrel), carried on between the English authorities and the French in Canada. The following is the record:

A SMALL TREASON IN BROOKLYN, BY SOME DUTCH CITIZENS, in 1696.

September 14.—About 8 o'clock in the evening, John Rapale, Isaac Remsen, Joseph Yannester, Joras Dainelse Rapale, Jacob Ryerson, Alert Aersen, Tunis Buys-Garret Cowenhoven, Gabriel Sprong, Urian Andres, John Williams Bennett, Jacob Bennett, and John Messerole, jr., met armed, at the Court House of Kings, where they destroyed and defaced the King's arms, which were hanging up there.

So you see there was rebellion in the blood of the settlers here, almost from the beginning.

In architecture we used to have a few notable specimens of early Dutch building existing in the City of Brooklyn, but we believe all are now removed. There is, however, one exception. Have our readers never heard or seen "the old iron 9's"?

This is the slang name among the boys of Brooklyn for probably the oldest house on Long Island, yet standing in Gowanus. It is in part stone and part brick, and was built in 1690 by Nicholas Vechte, and is known as the Cortelyou House. It was the headquarters of the commander-in-chief previous to the Battle of Long Island. The body of the house is of stone, the gable ends, above the eaves, of brick imported from Holland; and the date is in iron figures upon one gable end, in the mason work.

II

ORIGINAL STOCK OF KINGS COUNTY

FIRST DISCOVERY, 1609

SETTLEMENT—1613–1623

EMIGRATION OF WALLOONS

FIRST EUROPEAN CHILD, SARAH RAPELJE

TRADITIONS BY GENERAL JOHNSON

UNBIDDEN VISIT OF DUTCH GOVERNOR

ROMANTIC STORIES OF THE RAPELJES
AND JANSENS

INCIDENT OF PHYSICAL STRENGTH

RULEF VANBRUNT

DESCENDANTS OF THIS ORIGINAL STOCK

It is well known that the original stock of the settlement of Kings County was from Holland. We do not think, however, it is generally appreciated how superior in physical, moral and mental qualities, that original stock certainly was. Nor have our readers, probably, at least many of them, any definite and fixed dates in their minds of the settlement and growth of what is now our great city. To fill these deficiencies, we will devote this paper to those dates, and to some reminiscences handed down of the early stock.

The year 1609 was the era of the discovery of Brooklyn, and of Manhattan Island, by Hendrick Hudson, who was prosecuting a voyage of discovery, having for its main purpose the long-desired object of a direct western passage from Europe to the Indies. Hudson entered here and discovered the North River, Long Island, and what is now New York Island. His representations induced his employers, the Dutch, to take steps for the immediate occupation of the new region.

In 1613 there were four houses on Manhattan Island, occupied by Europeans—these were down toward where the Battery now is. By the succeeding year the new comers had ascended to what is now Albany, and built a strong edifice, called a "Block house" (Fort Nassau), for purposes of security and trade.

In 1614 the government of the Hague specifically claimed the whole territory between Canada and Virginia as theirs, under the name of the New Netherlands. This was the first determined official recognition.

In 1621 the States General gave a charter or act of incorporation to a powerful company under the name of the Dutch West India Company, who, among other franchises, were invested with full powers to govern the above-mentioned province. This was the commencement of the existence of Brooklyn as a political community.

11

The first serious attempt at planting a settlement here was in 1618. At that time the West India Company above named sent out a vessel from the Hague filled with emigrants to the Netherlands. These emigrants consisted mostly of Walloons, as they were called. Others followed—a vessel being dispatched every four or five months. In 1623, there were over two hundred European settlers in the colony, including those on Manhattan Island, and on this side of the river also—for all those who determined to settle here for good, for agricultural purposes, preferred Long Island to Manhattan, for obvious reasons.

Indeed there was no comparison between the two which was not obviously to the advantage of Long Island. It was fertile, beautiful, well-watered, and had plenty of timbers; while Manhattan was rocks, bare, bleak, and without anything to recommend it except its situation for commercial purposes, which is without rival in the world. The consequence was, as just intimated, that the best and permanent portion of the emigrants immediately fixed on this island, and settled in the neighborhood of what is now our "Wallabout."

In this Wallabout (Waalboght) region, in 1625, was born the first child of European parents, Sarah Rapelje. This fact is confirmed, inasmuch as some thirty years afterwards when Sarah had grown up to woman's estate, and had married, and then lost her husband, being left a widow with several children, she petitioned the municipal authorities for a grant of land, and it was given her, on the ground that she was the first born of the colony.

We will also relate in this connection a tradition which we have heard from Gen. Jeremiah Johnson, in reference to this Sarah Rapelje. We forget now the sources the General relied on for the legend.

When Sarah's father, George Jansen De Rapelje, was

settled on his farm in the Wallabout, Peter Minnet was Dutch governor in New Amsterdam, and lived on Manhattan Island. It happened one day that this governor, with several companions, crossed over to Long Island on a hunting excursion, and after a good tramp they found themselves extremely hungry in the neighborhood of Rapelje's house. This they entered in search of food and drink; but found nobody at all in the house, the wife with the rest being engaged at work out in the field. But Minnet and his friends had discovered a savory dish of "Indian dumplings"—the only thing apparently the larder contained—to which they helped themselves, and, constrained by their voracious appetites, made a clean dish of the whole fare. Just as they were concluding their repast, Frau Rapelje, with her little girl (Sarah) in her arms, returned from the field, to get ready the meal for husband and child. To her dismay and indignation she found the eatables the house had contained just devoured by the governor and his friends; and in her anger, and without the least respect for authority, she unloosed her woman's tongue, and gave them such a blast as only an enraged woman can. She particularly complained that when she had come home to feed her hungry child she found everything eaten up by great overgrown thieves and robbers! To pacify her, and make it all right, the governor, in the emergency, promised her that, if she would say no more about it, he would pledge his gubernatorial word that, in lieu of the dish of dumplings, he would, when the next ship came in, make the Frau a present of a good milch cow—which in due time he did, according to his promise.

Romantic stories were told in early times about these same Rapeljes. For George Jansen's two brothers came over here and settled also. One of the stories was that they were Moors by birth and of prodigious strength. As to birth, they were really the sons of French exiles, who had settled in the Low Countries, as often happened in those times. The reputed stature and strength of George Jansen's brother Antony were probably not without foundation. For according to Gen. Jeremiah Johnson, the grandson of this Antony, who lived in Gravesend, was six feet four inches high; and on one occasion, to give a sample of his bodily powers, he carried ten bushels of wheat from his barn to the house, and up the chamber stairs. Gen. Johnson said that, in his youth, he had visited and seen this grandson, whose name was William Jansen. Gen. J. inquired of him the truth of this story of carrying the ten bushels of wheat, and how he did it. William told his young visitor, "I took one bag on each shoulder, one in each hand, and one in my teeth"; and then opening the chamber door, he showed Gen. J. the stairs he had ascended, and the floor where he had deposited the wheat. This William lived to be 80 years of age, and died so late as 1805.

As another evidence that great bodily strength is hereditary in the line, Gen. Johnson mentioned that in the last war another descendant of this same Antony Jansen, by the name of Rulef Vanbrunt, in New Utrecht, caught two men stealing on his premises and on his confronting them, they attempted to attack him, but he gript one of the robbers in one hand, and one in the other, and thus bounced their heads to and to together, till, when he unloosed them, they were glad enough to run away as fast as their legs could carry them.

These Jansens all seem to have been a long-lived stock, and also to have had a faculty of adding largely to the population. The mother of the just-mentioned Rulef Vanbrunt was a grand-daughter of Antony Jansen, and was living a few years ago at New Utrecht, in the 95th year of her age—but has doubtless since deceased.

The families of Johnsons, Rapeljeas, Vanbrunts, etc.,

now so numerous in Brooklyn, and Kings County, are descended from this stock. The name of George Jansen's descendant soon changed to be written Rapelye, or Rapelyea. His brother Antony's descendants wrote their names Jansen, which has now for a long time been written Johnson.

Gen. Jeremiah Johnson was a lineal descendant in the fifth generation from Antony. It is a good stock, all round, and Kings County has no reason to be ashamed of it.

We shall continue the résumé of these incidents and dates in another number.

III

A SNOW SCENE IN BROOKLYN IN THE
OLDEN TIME

ANECDOTES OF THE PAINTER, FROM A
PERSONAL ACQUAINTANCE

THE LOCALITY OF THE PICTURE

THE FIGURE LIKENESSES

SOME OF THE OLD RESIDENCES OF
FRONT STREET

Among the few relics left to remind the present inhabitants of Brooklyn of the days and scenes of their grandfathers, few are more valuable than the large, somewhat time-stained picture known as "Guy's Brooklyn." This work is to be seen at the Brooklyn Institute, corner of Concord and Washington streets, and, though not attractive to the fashionable taste, will amply repay a visit from anyone who feels an interest in local antiquarianism. Soon after the painting was made, in the earliest part of the present century, it was exhibited here and in New York, under the title of "A Snow Scene in Brooklyn," by F. Guy, of Baltimore. We have heard from an old residenter, who personally knew this Guy, that the way he used to paint his pictures was in the following manner: A position and direction were fixed upon, looking out of a window if possible, and when the place to be pictured was well conned and determined, Guy would construct a large rough frame and fix it in the window, or in such a position that it enclosed in its view whatever he wished to portray—and outside of the frame all was shut off and darkened.

He would then rapidly sketch in his outline; and it was in this manner he prepared for painting the "Snow Scene." It was made, we have been informed, from one of the old houses still standing on the north side of Front Street, a hundred feet or thereabout east of Fulton.

Front Street at that time included some of the best dwellings in Brooklyn, those of the Grahams, Sandses, Birdsalls, etc. These fronted toward the south, and had large gardens, sloping northward down to the river, of which they had a beautiful open view, making altogether a charming and most picturesque situation.

This picture of Guy's, we believe, was thus a literal portrait of the scene as it appeared from his window there in Front Street, looking south. The houses and ground are thickly covered with snow. The villagers are around, in the performance of work, travel, conversation, etc. Some of the figures are likenesses. We have heard that the full-length portraits of Mr. Sands, Mr. Graham, Judge Garrison, Messrs. Titus Birdsall, Hicks, Meeker and Patchen, then leading townspeople here, are some of the principal ones in the composition.

The tract of surface represented is what now constitutes the sweep of Front Street, from Fulton to Main Street, and the region toward the south in the neighborhood of what is now Brooklyn market. As to time, it is a picture of some sixty years ago—a picture of a thriving semi-country cluster of houses in the depth of winter, with driving carts, sleighs, travelers, ladies, gossips, negroes (there were slaves here in those days), cattle, dogs, wheelbarrows, poultry, etc.—altogether a picture quite curious to stand on the same spot and think of now.

We have thus attempted to give a sketch of the spot and persons commemorated in the print from Guy's composition, which, though perhaps not of superior excellence in art, is still of great value as a reminiscence to all Brooklynites. Moreover, it is in some respects not without high merit simply as a piece of composition. Its perspective appears to be capital. The sky is also good in the original work. We will add that our informant before alluded to as a personal acquaintance of Guy's told us years ago that the painter was always aided and assisted by his wife—that she, in fact, was a woman of great energy and talent, and that this picture is probably as much indebted to her hands as to her husband's.

IV

COMPARISON OF BROOKLYN WITH THE
SETTLEMENTS OF NEW ENGLAND
AND VIRGINIA

THE INDIAN ABORIGINES—THE KANARSIES

REMNANTS EXISTING UNTIL LATELY

ORIGINAL SPELLING OF BROOKLYN

BUTTERMILK CHANNEL

ORIGINAL PRICE OF BEDFORD AND OF
NEW YORK ISLAND

FIRST TRADE OF NEW NETHERLANDS

IMPORTATIONS AND EXPORTS

PEACEFUL PURCHASES OF LAND

DESCRIPTION OF THE INDIAN MONEY,
OF WHICH LONG ISLAND WAS THE GREAT
MANUFACTORY FOR THE CONTINENT

A series of articles on Brooklyn with special reference to its origin and past history would hardly be complete without a glance at the conditions of this section of the island when it was first planted by the Dutch, with some brief mention of the natural advantages, etc., of the spot. The histories of our country have much to say on the subject of the Puritan foundation of New England, and the rival foundation in Virginia, with accounts of the tribes found there; and yet here on this island are some points of interest transcending either of those celebrated beginnings of European colonization.

If the reader will but carry his mind back to the times of the original settlement of Kings County (1614–50), he will easily perceive that there are many interesting circumstances connected with the locality, the original inhabitants, etc., etc.

When the Dutch first planted themselves here (and for some time afterward) the whole of Kings County was possessed and ruled by the Kanarsie tribe of Indians. The principal settlements were at Flatbush and, according to tradition, the locality toward the shore that still goes by the name of the tribe. In the latter spot was the residence of the sachem.

Our readers may not be aware that down to a comparatively late period of time remnants of this tribe still continued to exist in Kings County, and were occasionally seen as visitors, selling clams, fish, baskets, etc., in Brooklyn.— (Descendants of the Indians or half-breeds still remain on the east end of the island, around the neighborhood of Peconic Bay, and especially on the peninsula of Montauk. We have repeatedly seen them there; but we have never seen any of these Kanarsie remnants. The last one, we have heard old Brooklynites say, became extinct between forty and fifty years ago).

So, here these aborigines lived, on fish, clams, berries, wild fruits, and game.—They paid little attention to the

23

cultivation of the land, except, perhaps, a little corn. Besides
their canoes, of which some were large and of elegant work-
manship, and their bows and arrows, almost the only manufactures among them were stone hatchets, and rude vessels
of earth, hardened in the fire. And yet, they had one article
of manufacture which is deserving of special notice—an
article which made this specific portion of the New World
possess a character different from any other, and superior to
any other. We mean the manufacture of aboriginal money,
which we shall presently describe.

The produce of the settlements of the New Netherlands,
and of the station at Albany, were principally furs, peltries,
etc., with which the West India Company's return ships were
freighted. The commerce springing out of the settlement
increased regularly from the very outset, and with great
rapidity. From the years 1624 to 1635 the number of beaver
skins exported from New Amsterdam was 60,192, and of
other skins, 9,437, valued at 725,117 guilders.

Then the colony furnished a market for many products
of the mother country. Almost everything required by civ-
ilized tastes was for a long while imported—even to the
tiles for roofing the houses; of these latter, sufficient specimens even yet exist in the limits of Brooklyn and New York
to give the reader a visible demonstration of what they were.

Following the peaceful and prudent method of the Dutch,
the new comers made specific purchases of the land from
the aboriginal inhabitants, as their first move. Our records
have numerous evidences of these purchases, even yet.

Of the west of the island, in possession of the Kanarsie
tribe of Indians, though it would be interesting to some
degree to enter into an account of those aboriginal inhabitants at the time of the appearance of the *Half-moon* and
Hendrick Hudson in these waters, our time does not now
admit.

The name given to our city in old times spells in different modes. "Breukleyn" was a very common style still to be found in the old records. "Brookland" is another. Some have traced the etymology of the first of those terms to the *broken land* (namely the mixture of hill and dale), which characterizes the topography of our region of the island. Others have formed the cause of the record in the *brooks* of fresh water that used to ripple along the surface. As to these, and all other such explanations, we give them for the reader's amusement, without much reliance ourselves on any of them.

Among the differences in the character and "lay" of the land, especially of the shores, between the present day and the times following the original settlement, we will state, it is well known that even so late as the Revolutionary War cattle were driven across from Brooklyn, over what is now Buttermilk Channel, to Governor's Island—then Nutten Island. The deepening of this channel since is attributable to the carrying out and extension of the wharves and piers on both the New York and Brooklyn sides of the river, greatly narrowing it, and increasing the force of the currents.

As to the peaceful purchases before alluded to, they were repeated, in behalf of all parties who assumed to have any claim on the lands. Not only the Dutch purchased of the Indians, but when the English governors came into possession, they also purchased the same ground over again, and had deeds made out.—These deeds, and the considerations paid are, to modern ideas, extremely amusing. For instance, in 1625, the Dutch governor, Peter Minnet, purchased from the aborigines the whole of Manhattan Island, including all the land that now forms the City and County of New York, for sixty guilders (twenty-four dollars)! And in 1670, under the English, the authorities of Brooklyn purchased from the Indians the large tract comprising Bedford, and a large stretch towards Flatbush and Jamaica, for the following price: "100 guilders, *seawant,* half a tun of strong beer, three long-barrelled guns (with powder and lead proportionably), and 4 coats."

Our neighbors owning house lots in New York City, and those in Bedford, and about the Clove Road and East New York, can now tell on what foundation the title of their property actually rests. The purchase-money just mentioned contains the term "seawant." This was the name of the *Indian money,* of which this same region now comprised in Brooklyn (and indeed Long Island generally), appears to have been the principal manufactory for the whole continent. This supposition is warranted by many facts, among the rest that the principal Indian name that this end of the island went by, when discovered, meant, "the money-manufacturing island." This money was made from the shells of quahung (large round clams), and from those of the periwinkle, oyster, etc. The inside portion of these shells were broken, rubbed on stones, and worn down smooth into bead-shaped dried pieces, and then strung upon the sinews of animals, through holes bored through with sharp stones. These strings, braided together a hand's breadth, and of more or less length, were the celebrated "belt of wampum," or seawant. Three beads of this black money, and six of white, were equivalent to an English penny, or a Dutch stuyver.

The process of trade between the Indians and the settlers here and in New York was as follows: the Dutch and English sold to the Indians hatchets, hoes, combs, scissors, guns, black and red cloth, etc., and received the seawant shells, in strings or belts, for pay; and then in return bought furs, corn, venison, etc., and paid in seawant. The Indians laughed at the idea of gold or silver money and would not touch either. The seawant was also strung upon the persons of the savages, for ornament. It was the tribute paid by the Indians here, when conquered by the Six Nations, the Mohawks, etc., with whom the aborigines of Kings County had frequent wars.

These points are worth putting on record, when we remember that this island, and especially this end of it, surpassed all the continent in the permanent manufacture of this curious article.

V

THE BRITISH PRISON SHIPS OF 1776–1783

CAPTIVES FROM SEA AND LAND

PATRIOTISM—SCENE IN 1782

ANDROS' ACCOUNT OF THE MISERIES
ON BOARD

NUMBER OF THE MARTYRS—WHERE BURIED

RELICS GATHERED IN 1807

VAULT PREPARED AND DEAD
DEPOSITED, 1808

PROCESSION, CEREMONIES, ETC.

PRESENT CONDITION OF THE VAULT

The much-talked-of American prison ships of the Revolutionary War, four or five old hulks, strong enough to hold together, but condemned as unfit for sea purposes—which hulks the invading British army brought round and anchored in our river during the years 1776–7–8 and 9. It will be remembered that the British, after the disastrous (to the Americans) Battle of Brooklyn, took possession of the City of New York at the very commencement of the war, and held it to the end. As their naval power gave them every advantage here, they made this the depot of their troops, stores, etc., and the largest receptacle of the numerous American prisoners they took from time to time in battle.

The principal of these prison ships was the old *Jersey,* a large 74-gun frigate. She was dismantled and moored on a spot now included in the dry land of our Brooklyn Navy Yard. Others lay off what is now the Battery. Then there were others, off and on; the *Whitby* (she was the first, and was burnt toward the latter part of the year 1777); the *Scorpion,* the *Good Hope* (!), the *Hunter,* and the *Stromboli* were the names of the others, or most of them. But the one which seems to have been most relied on was the old *Jersey.*

The British took a great many American prisoners during the war—not only by land, but also by their privateers, at sea. When a capture was made in any of the waters near enough, the prisoners were brought with the vessel to New York. These helped to swell the rank of the unhappy men, who were crowded together in the most infernal quarters, starved, diseased, helpless, and many becoming utterly desperate and insane.—Death and starvation killed them off rapidly.

The *Scorpion, Stromboli,* and *Hunter* were called hospital ships—but mighty little health was there on any of the others. The American Government, after a while, appointed

31

commissioners who, by consent of the British generals, were permitted to visit New York and contribute to the relief of the prisoners—but they could only advance a very moderate degree of assistance. The British put out the keeping of the prisoners by contract, and as there was no one to look after the contractors, and their jobs were like all such favoritism, they made fortunes out of the starvation of thousands of unhappy men. The food was often the refuse of the English soldiery and of the ships of war in commission. There was the most frightful suffering from the want of water. The air was fetid, in warm weather, to suffocation. Still with all these facts, these thousands of men, any one of whom might have had his liberty by agreeing to join the British ranks, sternly abided by their fate and adhered to the cause of their country to the bitter end.

The patriotism of these prisoners appeared indeed to be all the more intense from their wrongs. On the anniversary of the Fourth of July, one time (1782), they resolved to celebrate the occasion as well as they could. They arranged and exhibited among themselves thirteen little flags, sung the patriotic songs of those times, (and there were many such in circulation in those days, with others also on the British side, deriding Americans), and occasionally joined in giving hearty rounds of cheers for the day, till at last the angry British guards drove them all below, and fastened the gratings upon them. Irritated at this, the prisoners raised their songs louder than ever, when the infuriated guards rushed down, charging in on the unarmed crowd, with fixed bayonets. Many were wounded frightfully, and several killed in the melee.

One of the prisoners on the old *Jersey,* after the end of the war, when he was liberated, wrote an account of the proceedings aboard this ship, and published it in a book. This was Thomas Andros, who was a great patriot, and after-

wards settled as minister of a church in Berkley, Massachu-
setts. According to his account, there were a thousand men
confined much of the time on the old *Jersey*—sometimes
increased to as many as twelve hundred. And as, at that
time, the hospital ships had also become overcrowded, the
sick were no longer removed from the *Jersey* but remained
with the rest. The following extract from Andros' account
seems to us interesting in the greatest degree, especially to
us who live in the neighborhood of the scene:

In a short time we had two hundred men, sick and dying, lodged in
the fore part of the lower gun deck, where all the prisoners were confined at night. Utter derangement was a common symptom of yellow
fever, and to increase the horror of the darkness which surrounded us,
(for we were allowed no light between decks), the voice of warning
could be heard: "Take heed to yourselves, there is a madman stalking
through the ship with a knife in his hand." I sometimes found the man
a corpse in the morning, by whose side I laid myself down at night.
At another time he would become deranged, and attempt in the darkness to rise, and stumble over the bodies that everywhere covered the
deck. In this case I tried to hold him in his place by main strength.
In spite of my efforts he would sometimes rise, and then I had to close
in with him, trip up his heels, and lay him again upon the deck. While
so many men were sick with raging fever, there was a loud cry for
water, but none could be had except on the upper deck, and but one
allowed to ascend at a time. The suffering then from the rage of
thirst was very great. Nor was it at all times safe to attempt to go up.
Provoked by the continual cry for leave to ascend when there was
already one on deck, the sentry would push them back with his bayo-
net. By one of these thrusts more spiteful and violent than common,
I had a narrow escape of my life. In the morning the hatchways were
thrown open, and we were allowed to ascend all at once, and remain
on the upper deck during the day. But the first object that met our
view in the morning was a most appaling spectacle—a boat loaded
with dead bodies, conveying them to the Long Island shore where they
were very slightly covered with sand. I sometimes used to stand to

count the number of times the shovel was filled with sand to cover a
dead body. And certain I am that a few high tides or torrents of rain
must have disinterred them. And had they not been removed, I should
suppose the shore even now would be covered with huge piles of the
bones of American seamen. There were probably four hundred on
board who never had the small-pox; some perhaps might have been
saved by inoculation. But humanity was wanting to try even this ex-
periment. Let our disease be what it would we were abandoned to our
fate. Now and then an American physician was brought as a captive,
but if he could obtain his parole, he left the ship, nor could we blame
him much for this, for his own death was next to certain, and his
success in saving others by medicine in our situation was very small.
I remember only two American physicians who tarried on board a few
days. No English physicians, or any one from the city, ever to my
knowledge came near us. There were thirteen of the crew to which I
belonged, but in a short time all but three or four were dead.

The most healthy and vigorous were last seized with the fever and
died in a few hours. For them there seemed to be no mercy. My constitution was less muscular and phlethoric, and I escaped the fever
longer than any of the thirteen except one, and the first onset was less
violent.

Most of the crowding of the prisoners, and the more
odious part of the treatment occurred in the earlier years
of the war. Toward the last the British themselves appear
to have grown ashamed and shocked at the proceedings of
their officers. The Americans also indignantly interfered and
produced a change toward the last.

The whole number of those who died aboard these ships
of death is reliably computed as close on twelve thousand
men, mostly in the flower of their age. It is a profound reflection that Brooklyn, in its Wallabout region, holds the
remains of this vast and silent army. Few think as they cross
the City Park, or pass along Flushing Avenue, of the scenes
here witnessed in the early part of our national history.

All the terra-firma of the present Navy Yard, and much of

the land adjoining it also, has since been reclaimed from the dominion of old Neptune—that is, it has been "filled in." Of course, the whole face of the scene has been completely changed from what it was in the times of the Revolutionary War, when the ships lay here. At that period, the spot that is now just west of the wall along Flushing Avenue was a low stretching sand hill, and it was in and adjacent to this spot that the thousands of the American martyrs were mostly buried. They were dumped in loose loads every morning in pits, and the sand shoveled over them. The writer of these lines has been told by old citizens that nothing was more common in their early days than to see thereabout plenty of the skulls and other bones of these dead— and that thoughtless boys would kick them about in play. Many of the martyrs were so insecurely buried that the sand, being blown off by the wind, exposed their bleached skeletons in great numbers.

The work of "filling in" here, for the purpose of completing the Government Navy Yard, commenced 1807-8. And it was at this time that public attention (and even public decency) were directed to some means of preservation, beyond the destiny of common rubbish, of these patriotic relics. Garret Sickles and Benjamin Romaine, of New York City (we believe Mr. R. afterward came to be a resident of Brooklyn), were prominent in the good work. At their instigation, the Tammany Society of New York made a formal business of it. Large quantities of loose and disjointed bones were collected, and it was determined to deposit them in a spot near at hand, deeded to the Tammany Society for that purpose by John Jackson, Esq. (from whom the old name of Jackson Street, and not from Gen. Jackson, as generally supposed). A vault was constructed here, a corner stone prepared, and the occasion was made one of the most imposing and expensive ceremonies, very disproportionate to the present appearance of the "temple," or "ante-chamber," now visible over this vault to the passer-by along Hudson Avenue, adjacent to the Navy Yard wall.

The ceremony alluded to consisted of two parts, one on the 12th of April, 1808, and a following one on the 26th of May. The first was the formal laying of the corner stone of the existing vault. A procession was formed at the Fulton Ferry, composed of United States marines, under command of their officers, and of the Tammany Society, and various civic societies, who proceded to the ground, where an oration was delivered by Joseph D. Fay, and then the corner stone was duly lowered in its place—on it being cut the following inscription:

IN THE NAME OF THE SPIRIT OF THE DEPARTED

Free, Sacred to the memory of that portion of American Seamen, Soldiers, and citizens, who perished on board the Prison Ships at the Wallabout, during the Revolution; This corner stone of the vault is erected by the Tammany Society, or Columbian Order; Nassau Island, Season of Blossoms, year of Discovery the 316th and of the institution the 19th and of American Independence the 32nd.

Jacob Vandervoort, John Jackson, Burdett Stryker, Issachar Cozzens, Robert Townsend, Jr., Benjamin Watson, Samuel Cowdry, Committee. David and William Campbell, Builders.

April 6, 1808.

But on the 26th of May following a still larger demonstration (the second part) was made. This was in the form of a procession to escort the relics of the martyrs to their place of burial, and deposit them there. Various societies and military companies met in the Park, in front of the City Hall, in New York, in the forenoon, under the direction of Brigadier-Generals Jacob Morton and Gerard Steddiford, and of Garret Sickles, Grand Marshal. A very lengthy and imposing procession was then formed with much of heraldic device and, it must be confessed, theatrical accompaniment. This lengthy procession was preceded, for instance, by a trumpeter, dressed in deep black, on a black horse, with trailing plumes and a black silk flag on his trumpet, with the following motto:

> Mortals, avaunt! 11,500 spirits of the murdered brave,
>   approach the tomb of honor, of glory, and of patriotism!

Of course the "cap of liberty" bore a conspicuous part in the show. In the 10th section of the cortege were thirteen coffins, significant of the martyrs from the old Thirteen States. These were attended by one hundred and four Revolutionary characters, as pall-bearers. This must have been the most impressive part of the procession. In another and following section was a "grand national pedestal," bearing the American flag, on the top of which staff was a globe, on which sat a bald eagle, enveloped in black crepe. This pedestal was rather a formidable affair; in front it had the inscription, "Americans, remember the British." On the right side, "Youth of my country! Martyrdom prefer to Slavery." On the left side, "Sires of Columbia! transmit to posterity the cruelties practiced on board the British Prison Ships." On the rear,

> Tyrants dread the gathering storm
> While freemen freemen's obsequies perform.

In another part of the procession were Gov. Daniel D. Tompkins, with members of the Legislature and Congress— and in another, the Mayor of New York, Dewitt Clinton, with members of the Common Council. The Freemasons, the Tammany Society, the clergy, the shipwrights, the Hibernian Society, the societies of tailors, hatters, coopers, etc., etc., all had places in the line. It must have been a very great affair indeed, for those days—for New York had not then seen any of the mighty turn outs, such as these characteristic of modern times.

All the above procession crossed to Brooklyn, by slow degrees in barges, and then re-formed and marched up through Sands Street to the location of the vault, where it now is on Hudson Avenue. The music of the bands, when the skeleton relics were taken in the line, was of the most mournful description. The sentiment of the occasion became overwhelmingly sorrowful and impressive. Many a one was in tears.

On the ground, after the relics were deposited, an oration was delivered by Dr. Benjamin Dewitt. The huge coffins containing the remains were then gazed upon in silence by the immense crowd, who soon slowly and gradually dispersed.

Of the vault thus canonized by a great and expensive ceremony, it appears to have remained ever since without anything further being done—except that, some time afterward, the title falling into the hands of Mr. Benjamin Romaine, before alluded to (who had himself, when a young man, been one of the American prisoners in the old *Jersey*), he had a temporary "Ante-Chamber," of wood, constructed, with an inscription, at considerable length, to commemorate the facts set forth in the foregoing article. This wooden structure, in a ruinous condition, still exists. We have been informed that such was the deep feeling which Mr. R. had about these relics, and the reminiscences connected with them, that he expressly provided in his will that his own remains should be deposited with them in the vault—and that they now rest there, his executors having obeyed his wishes.

At one time and another, there have been movements

made for putting up some memorial worthy of the martyrs of the prison ships, in Brooklyn. The one most likely to be carried out, when a favorable period occurs, is that for raising an appropriate monument on the highest point of old Fort Greene, Washington Park. If this is ever done, we hope it will not be spoilt by adopting any such absurd designs as by some adverse fates have been fixed upon all other American monuments—the Washington monument at the Capital—the Worth monument, in Fifth Avenue, New York—and even the chimney-shaped Bunker Hill monument, in Boston.

ADDITIONAL

The little old wooden "temple," the only existing memorial of the martyrs of the prison ships, is in Hudson Avenue (formerly Jackson Street), between the line of the street and the Navy Yard wall.

Since the preceding part of our article on the prison ships was written, we have gleaned one or two additional items that we dare say our readers will find of interest on this subject.

The water that supplied the *Jersey,* and the other old hulks used as prison ships at the Wallabout, 1776–'82, was brought from a spring near what is now Kent Avenue, but a few rods from the well-known residence of Barnet Johnson —at that day approached by a creek much nearer than at present. Between this spring and the hulks, a water-boat was kept constantly plying, as thirst was indeed the greatest torment of the crowded prisoners.

On the *Jersey,* it is recorded that a resolute guard, with drawn cutlasses, was kept over the water-butts constantly, the regulation being that no prisoner should be permitted to help himself to more than a pint of water in his turn.

FOURTH OF JULY, 1782

We alluded in the first part of this article to the attempt of the prisoners at the Wallabout, in 1782, to commemorate the Fourth of July. The British guards and officers were so enraged at this that they drove the prisoners below at four o'clock in the afternoon, instead of leaving them their usual privileges on deck till sunset. This treatment irritated the Americans to such a degree that they kept up their patriotic songs and cheers, down in their close and hot confinement. An hour or two after dark, the guard came down, attended by some holding lanterns; and with fixed bayonets they charged right and left on the compact mass of prisoners, after which cowardly exploit they returned again to the upper deck.

This must have been a most lamentable night. It was described afterwards by Thomas Dring, one of the prisoners who lived through it, in the following terms:

Of this night I can hardly describe the horrors. The day had been very sultry, and the heat was extreme throughout the ship. The unusual number of hours we had been congregated together between decks, the foul atmosphere and sickening heat, the additional excitement and restlessness caused by the wanton attack which had been made—above all, the want of water, not a drop of which could be obtained during the whole night to cool our parched tongues; the imprecations of those who were half distracted with their burning thirst; the shrieks and wailings of the wounded, with the struggles and groans of the dying, together formed a combination of horrors which no pen can describe.

At length the morning light began to dawn, but still our torments increased every moment. As the usual hour for us to ascend to the upper deck approached, the "working party" were mustered near the hatchway, and we were all anxiously waiting for the opportunity to cool our weary frames, to breathe for a while the pure air, and, above all to procure water to quench our intolerable thirst. The time arrived, but still the gratings were not removed. Hour after hour passed on, and still we were not released.

Our minds were at length seized with a horrible suspicion that our tyrants had determined to make a finishing stroke of their cruelty, and rid themselves of us altogether. But about 10 o'clock that forenoon the gratings were removed.

We hurried on deck and thronged to the water cask, which was completely exhausted before our thirst was allayed. So great was the struggle around the cask that the guards were turned out to disperse the crowd.

Not until long after the usual hour were our rations delivered to us. During the whole day, however, no fire was kindled in the galley. All the food which we consumed that day we were obliged to swallow raw.

The number of dead found that morning was ten.

Such in the words of one who was afterwards a citizen of the United States, gives a specimen night and day aboard one of these Wallabout prison ships, the old *Jersey*, during the Revolutionary War. This old *Jersey* held about 1,000 prisoners at that time. Sometimes fifty or sixty would be carried off by death in the course of the week.

OF THE "TEMPLE"

When Mr. Romaine had the temporary mausoleum built, he had it covered with such inscriptions as the following, now rendered almost illegible:

In 1778, the Confederation proclaimed thirteen British colonies, United States—E Pluribus Unum. In 1783 our grand National Convention ordained one entire Sovereignty, in strict adhesion to the equall[y] sacred State Rights.

The Constitution of the United States consists of two parts—the Supreme Sovereignty, and the un[a]dulterated State Rights, one and indivisible.

In the city of New York, 1783, Washington began the first Presidential career—the wide spread eagle of Union [a]waited the order, then instantly raised his flight in the heavens, and like the orb of day, speedily became visible to half the globe.

We have remarked in what a ruinous and sluttish condition the only existing memorial of the martyrs now exists. Just at present is not the time for inaugurating any expensive enterprise, but we hope that when the affairs and business of the country return to the usual prosperous channels, some effective means will be taken to redeem the disgraceful neglect that has too long continued in regard to putting up some enduring and appropriate memorial to the martyrs of the prison ships.

VI

THE FIRST BROOKLYN NEWSPAPER

THOMAS KIRK

WILLIAM HARTSHORNE, THE VETERAN OF
UNITED STATES PRINTERS

EARLY TYPESETTING EXPERIENCE

THE *LONG ISLAND PATRIOT*, MR. BIRCH

S. E. CLEMENTS

JUDGE ROCKWELL

PECULIARITIES OF PRINTING THE PAPER
AND SERVING SUBSCRIBERS

Among the most significant hints of the difference between these days of 1862 and the days from 1830, and so on backward to 1800, would be those furnished by looking over some volume of newspapers published between the two last-mentioned dates. To people who have not availed themselves of the opportunity of such an examination, it would be almost incredible what a "great gulf" there is between the press of the present day, and a New York or Brooklyn newspaper of that aforesaid period.

As we have never been able to procure or get sight of a copy of the very first newspaper established in Brooklyn, we have long ago made up our mind that there is probably no copy of that paper in existence. Still, there *may* be some preserved somewhere, in old records or perhaps garret rubbish —and they may turn up yet, to gladden the eyes of antiquarians, and give point to local contrasts and reminiscences. We have now within reach of the hand that is writing these lines a copy of the *New York Mercury,* printed in 1760, some fifteen years before the commencement of the Revolutionary War, and "containing the freshest advices foreign and domestick,"—but, as we said, although there are many files and odd numbers of old New York and New England newspapers preserved in one place and another, there are none, as far as we have yet been able to trace them, of any of the aforementioned first newspapers printed in Brooklyn. Or possibly the publication of these lines may succeed in bringing to light some odd number or numbers of such antique print.

The first newspaper printed in Brooklyn was in 1729. It was called the *Courier and Long Island Advertizer.* The venerable William Hartshorne (a most worthy member of the craft preservative of all crafts), to whom we are indebted for our information, was present at the first issue of this paper. Of its history, appearance, peculiarities, etc., we are unable to give any detailed account at present—except that it was published, and had a job-printing office attached to it, for some six or seven years; and at the end of that time its proprietor, Mr. Thomas Kirk, either abandoned the publication of the *Courier* altogether, or else, for some reason or other, transformed it into another paper, called the *Long Island Star*.

One old aboriginal Brooklyn newspaper, however, we have seen, that was published as far back as 1808, by parties who seem to have been competitors with Mr. Kirk. This is called the *Long Island Weekly Intelligencer,* conducted by Robinson & Little. The printing office announces itself as at the corner of Old Ferry and Front Streets. (By Old Ferry our readers will understand the present Fulton Street.) This number publishes the list of letters remaining in the post office uncalled for for the previous three months. The list comprises about fifty letters.

It must have been in 1808 or 9 that the old *Long Island Star* was first issued by Thomas Kirk. It was a small weekly, and gave what would now be called very meagre gleanings of current news, old political intelligence, jokes, scraps of items, and advertisements of local wants, etc. Among others, may be noticed the hiring of slaves, both male and female. For we suppose our readers are aware of the fact that it is but a little while since slavery existed here in this very town, and all through Long Island, and all over the state.

Scant and poor, however, as was the literary nutriment presented by one of these old weekly issues, it was eagerly sought for by the limited reading public of those days, and welcomed and conned over with perhaps just as much satisfaction as the full-blown modern daily or weekly now is by its readers. Those were the days when "literature" had not become the dissipation which our modern days have created.

We have spoken of William Hartshorne—he was the

veteran printer of the United States. His quiet life, and his never having taken a part in momentous affairs of any kind, make it impossible that he should ever have a biography— but he deserves one full as much as more eminent persons. He died a little over a year ago, at the age of 84, having lived in Brooklyn some 65 years. He came here from Philadelphia, a little before the close of the last century. He remembered well, and has many a time described to the writer hereof (who listened with a boy's ardent soul and eager ears), the personal appearance and demeanor of Washington, Jefferson, and other of the great historical names of our early national days.

Mr. Hartshorne had a very good memory, with an intellect bright, even in his old age, and was willing, to an appreciative listener, to give copious reminiscences of the personages, things, and occurrences, of 70, 60, or 50 years ago, and so on downwards to later times. In worldly circumstance he held that position in life which consists of neither poverty nor riches. He had the old school manner, rather sedate, not fast, never too familiar, always restraining his temper, always cheerful, benevolent, friendly, observing all the decorums of language and action, square and honest, invariably temperate, careful in his diet and costume, a keeper of regular hours—in bodily appearance a small man, hair not very grey, and though not at all of robust habit of body (indeed rather fragile), and of a trade considered unhealthy, he lived to the extended age of eighty-four years.

In 1831 Mr. Hartshorne occupied part of an old Revolutionary building in Fulton Street, east side, third door below Nassau Street, in the basement of which he had a small printing office of a few printer's stands, etc., where he set up type for a weekly newspaper (printed up stairs), and he also kept a small stationery store. It was in the just mentioned year that the writer hereof (then a boy of 12 years), received from Mr. H. in the little office in the basement of that old Revolutionary house, with its brick walls and its little narrow doors and windows, the first instructions in type-setting—the initiation into the trade and mystery of our printing craft.

What compositor, running his eye over these lines, but will easily realize the whole modus of that initiation?—the half eager, half bashful beginning—the awkward holding of the stick—the type-box, or perhaps two or three old cases, put under his feet for the novice to stand on, to raise him high enough—the thumb in the stick—the compositor's rule—the upper case almost out of reach—the lower case spread out handier before him—learning the boxes—the pleasing mystery of the different letters, and their divisions —the great 'e' box—the box for spaces right by the boy's breast—the 'a' box, 'i' box, 'o' box, and all the rest—the box for quads away off in the right hand corner—the slow and laborious formation, type by type, of the first line—its unlucky bursting by the too nervous pressure of the thumb —the first experience in 'pi,' and the distributing thereof— all this, I say, what journeyman typographer cannot go back in his own experience and easily realize?

As for William Hartshorne, for the fifteen or twenty years previous to his death, the old man was often to be seen walking slowly in pleasant weather, through Fulton Street, or some neighboring thoroughfare, with broad-brim hat, his cane, and chewing his quid of tobacco. For our own part, we used always to stop and salute him, with good-will and reverence. And so, age and decay creeping on, after a stretch of longevity very remarkable for a printer, in December 1859, the venerable man died, probably the oldest, most remarkable, and certainly one of the most upright and intelligent, of the working printers of the United States.

We don't know at what year the publication here in

Brooklyn of the *Long Island Patriot* was commenced, but we remember the paper well, and held for a time the distinguished position of one of the juvenile devils, so important to its concoction and general manufacture. This was after our initiation by Mr. Hartshorne. Of the previous fortunes of the *Patriot,* we know not, except that it was the original Democratic organ of Kings County. We remember Mr. Birch, its first proprietor, very well, and we remember the paper equally well—for the male parent hereof was one of its steady patrons from the beginning. The paper was left for its subscribers with great care, each one's name being written on the edge. We remember seeing the aforesaid male parent's name plainly written on the *Patriot* as it was left every week at the house. This paper, and those previous, and indeed for a while afterwards were all printed on old-fashioned wooden hand-presses, an edition of a few hundred copies being considered fully satisfactory. It was not an uncommon thing for the editor and proprietor of the paper to serve them with care to the subscribers through the town with his own hands.

Early in Jackson's administration, Mr. Birch sold out his concern to Samuel E. Clements, a very tall and eagle-nosed Southerner, who was also appointed post master, and occupied for his printing establishment and his post office the old Revolutionary building aforementioned. The *Patriot* (the name was changed not long after to the *Brooklyn Advocate*), continued to be the Democratic and Jackson organ. Political excitement and partisan fury ran just as high then as now. It was the time of the great contest between Old Hickory and the United States Bank.

In addition to the above reminiscences of the press, and of its publishers and printers here in Brooklyn, we may mention that the late Judge Rockwell succeeded S. E. Clements as editor of the *Patriot,* and continued it as a Democratic weekly paper—and that subsequently a Mr. Douglas purchased the paper and changed its name—as above mentioned—to the *Brooklyn Advocate*.

Mr. Hartshorne was at one time appointed by a vote of the Common Council to the post of city printer, and continued for several years to print the pamphlets, blanks, handbills, etc., for the city departments.

Between '30 and '40, two or three attempts were made to establish daily papers in Brooklyn, but they only lost money to their projectors.

VII

POPULATION

DEFECTIVENESS OF THE LATE CENSUS

BROOKLYN WELL KNOWN ABROAD

LIST OF THE MANUFACTURES
AND PRODUCTS

EDIFICES

CAPITAL

STOCK COMPANIES

SURFACE SITUATION OF BROOKLYN

OURS IS TO BE A CITY OF OVER
A MILLION INHABITANTS.

PRIVATE DWELLINGS

We will occupy this paper of our series with some remarks on the situation, advantages, healthiness, etc., of Brooklyn —and with a bird's eye view of its manufacturing industry. Probably, in both particulars, the very citizens that live in our midst pass on their way from year to year without giving a thought on the subject.

Our population is probably this day fully 300,000 persons —although the census summer before last puts the number considerably below that. To our personal knowledge, however, that census was taken in the most defective manner.

It may not be generally known that our city is getting to have quite a world-wide reputation, and that it is not unfrequently specified, as a familiar name in the Old World, in the discussions there, in their literary periodicals. We noticed, for instance, in a leading article in the great London *Times*, in a number dated about a month since, that tycoon of the European press alluded to the City of Brooklyn, to point one of its illustrations—as if the name and facts of the said city would be familiar enough to its readers through the British islands, and on the continent.

And now to our manufactures.

Few persons have any idea of the immense variety of manufactures, works, foundries, and other branches of useful art and trade carried on in the limits of our expansive and thriving city. For illustration, we will append a list of manufactures (many of which we have at one time or another personally visited), and all of them in operation now in different parts of our city. It will, we are sure, be quite a curiosity to many of our readers:

ANNUAL MANUFACTURES AND PRODUCTS OF BROOKLYN, ACCORDING TO THE STATE CENSUS, 1855, (NOW LARGELY INCREASED, AND WITH NEW BRANCHES, PROBABLY DOUBLE.)

Market produce . .	$120,078		Lager beer . . .	750,000
Ag. Implements .	30,000		Stoves	85,000
Brass & copper			Steam engines . .	75,000
foun'ds . . .	400,000		Ship's blocks . . .	70,000
Silver plating . .	7,000		Ship building . .	945,000
Bronze castings . .	26,000		Steamboat finishing	150,000
Copper-smithing .	375,000		Tree nails . . .	20,000
Fish-hooks . . .	10,000		Thermometers . .	1,500
Furnaces	9,000		Sashes and blinds .	120,000
Gold and silver re-			Coaches and	
fining	224,000		wagons . . .	70,000
Iron pipe	350,000		Registers and	
Francis' metallic			ventilators . .	100,000
life boats . . .	80,000		Pumps	15,000
Safes	200,000		Steam pumps . .	200,000
Silver ware . . .	60,000		Flour and feed . .	1,000,000
Tin and sheet iron	150,000		Packing boxes . .	25,000
Wire sieves . . .	25,000		Casks and barrels .	13,000
Cotton batting . .	75,000		Planed boards . .	500,000
Felting and			Camphe[n]e . .	2,000,000
wadding . . .	5,000		Chemicals . . .	60,000
Dressed flax . . .	6,000		Refined sugar and	
Fringes and tassels .	40,000		syrup	2,000,000
Dressed furs . . .	120,000		Confectionary . .	20,000
Paper	20,000		Drugs and medicines	15,000
Rope and cordage .	2,500,000		Dyewood	100,000
Twine and nets . .	12,000		Fish and whale oil	200,000
Gas	462,000		Lamps, lanterns, &	
Glue	150,000		gas fixtures . .	125,000
Distilled liquors .	6,000,000		Ivory black and	
Clocks	16,000		bone manure . .	110,000
Pianos	250,000		Japanned cloth . .	200,000
Brown powder . .	10,000		Lamp-black . . .	4,000

Soap and candles .	250,000	Lard oil	10,000
Refined liquorice .	50,000	Shingles	10,000
Malt	100,000	Veneering . . .	16,000
Oil cloth	200,000	Glassware . . .	800,000
Linseed and other		Lime	12,000
oil	300,000	Marble	100,000
Paints and colors .	54,000	Cut stone . . .	250,000
osiu [sic] oil . .	25,000	Leather (ordinary)	50,000
Kerosene	200,000	Patent leather . .	250,000
Saleratus	50,000	Morocco	2,000,000
Starch	30,000	Paper hangings . .	30,000
Vinegar	12,000	Rugs and mats . .	100,000
White lead . . .	1,250,000	Window shades .	50,000
Whiting	68,000	Gold pens . . .	100,000
		Hats and caps . .	100,000
		Tobacco and cigars	200,000

This is all that is given in the last state census.

But large as the foregoing list is, it leaves out unmentioned very many of the principal productive interests of Brooklyn, such as those giving employment to housebuilders, the cartmen, drivers, City Railroad employees, etc., etc. There were in 1855 the number of 22,573 buildings in Brooklyn. Of these 511 were of stone, valued at $5,000,000; and 8,039 were of brick, valued at $40,000,000. The rest were, of course, wooden edifices, and were valued at $30,000,000.

Of the foregoing list, several points in connection may be here mentioned. The manufacturing of hats is put at far too low a figure. There is one establishment alone in the city that turned out, either then, or immediately afterward, probably twice or three times that amount of work—to say nothing of numerous other large hat factories. Of the distilleries, one of the largest, when in full operation, absorbs 3000 bushels of grain per day. There are about ten rope-walks,

employing from ten to fifteen hundred men and boys. There
are from fifteen to twenty breweries in the eastern district,
in the neighborhood of Bushwick; these are the sources of
the mighty outpourings of ale and lager beer, refreshing the
thirsty lovers of those liquids in hot or cold weather. There
are eight or ten ship-yards at Greenpoint, employing from
five to seven hundred men, when in operation. Brooklyn has
the only plate-glass manufactory in the United States. The
white lead factory gives employment to two hundred and
twenty-five men. Immense quantities of spirits are shipped
direct from the distilleries here to France (to return, we
suppose, in the shape of pure French brandies, wines, etc.).

We can only hint at, without specifying, the immense
amounts of capital employed here in the bank, insurance
offices, the Union Ferry Company, the Brooklyn City Railroad Company, the Central, the Long Island Railroad (capital of the latter $3,000,000), and the Atlantic Dock
Improvements, the gas companies, and the immense and in
every way triumphant Brooklyn Water Works.

Our Navy Yard also employs 3000 men, and turns out
works to the annual amount of tens of millions of dollars.

And now a few words on our geographical situation, etc.

The topography of the City of Brooklyn is very fine. Indeed it is doubtful if there is a city in the world with a better
situation for beauty, or for utilitarian purposes. As to its
healthiness, it is well known. No wonder it took the eyes of
the early Holland immigrants. It is hilly and elevated in its
natural state—and these peculiarities, graded down somewhat by the municipal improvements, but still preserved in
their essential particulars, give us a sight of unsurpassed
advantage and charming scenery. With much greater attrac-
tions for residence than our neighboring island of New
York, Brooklyn is steadily drawing hither the best portion
of the business population of the great adjacent metropolis,

who find here a superior place for dwelling. So that it is not at all improbable that, at the end of the century, we may have here a larger number of inhabitants than will be eventually within the limits of New York City.

We have now marked advantages for residents. There is the best quality and cheapest priced gas—the best water in the world—a prospect of moderate taxation—and, we will say, for our city authorities, elected year after year, that they will compare favorably with any of similar position in the United States. Much slang is always expended on city officials—but as to ours, they are generally men of probity and intelligence, and perform their duties to the public satisfaction.

Why then should not Brooklyn, in the experience of persons now living, become a city of a great million inhabitants? We have no doubt it will. We can not go over the list and description of our public institutions in this paper, although we intend to do so one of these days. We have not, in a modern city like Brooklyn, such marked specimens of magnificent architecture as the ancient or mediaeval cities presented, and many of whose ruins yet remain. For *our* architectural greatness consists in the hundreds and thousands of superb private dwellings, for the comfort and luxury of the great body of middle class people—a kind of architecture unknown until comparatively late times, and no where known to such an extent as in Brooklyn, and the other first class cities of the New World.

Still, we have some public edifices creditable in a high degree. The City Hall is a handsome structure enough. Several of the churches are noble buildings, and the new Academy of Music is a sufficient success in an architectural point of view outside. But, after all, there are private rows of buildings in some of the choice streets of our city that transcend any single public edifice among us that we know of.

The reservoirs of our water works, and the buildings connected with them, and some of the monuments in Greenwood Cemetery, are worthy of being specially mentioned before conclusion.

VIII

SITE OF THE ACADEMY OF MUSIC

FIRST BROOKLYN THEATRE, 1828,
AND ITS FAILURE

BROOKLYN MUSEUM AND ITS
MANAGEMENT

OLD-TIME AMUSEMENTS

CELEBRATIONS

A FOURTH OF JULY PATRIOTISM

RECEPTION OF LAFAYETTE IN
BROOKLYN, 1825

THE BOYS AND GIRLS

Now that we have our magnificent *Academy of Music,* so beautiful outside and in, and on a scale commensurate with similar buildings, even in some of the largest and most pollished capitals of Europe, it will not be amiss to recur to what our city has had, in former times, of theatres, and places of kindred amusement.

The same neighborhood—indeed the very locality—occupied by this temple of Italian song has many a time, in former years, been covered over with the circus-tent, barricaded with big baggage-wagons and iron-grated cages of animals belonging to some perambulating "show." These circus exhibitions, by the way, have alway been a sure card in Brooklyn. The proprietors have repeatedly told us that they have always relied on making up for slim attendance elsewhere by "full houses" here—and have never been disappointed.

Probably very few of the readers who peruse these lines will be aware that we had a very handsome and respectable theatre put up in Brooklyn as early as 1828. Yet such is the case; and it would not have made a discreditable show, even for the requirements of the present time. It was a large and neat wooden edifice, and stood on the east side of Fulton Street, immediately below Concord. It was so arranged in its interior that it could be changed in a few moments from a theatrical stage into accommodations for a circus, or vice versa. It had three tiers of boxes, and was about as large and convenient as the "old Richmond Hill," the play-house which stood, and was popular some years ago in Varick Street, New York.

For some reason or other, however, the Brooklyn theatre we speak of never "took" very well. There were performances there, but with long intervals between; one or two attempts being made to get up rather showy "horse spectacles," of the style of "Timour the Tartar," etc., but they were received with chilliness by the Brooklyn public of those times. The corps of actors and actresses were of a very inferior order; and consequently the more educated families of our town avoided the place on play-nights. It therefore soon became resigned to audiences of a third-rate description at very cheap prices, and thus declined and died.

The edifice, not paying for the purposes originally contemplated, was transformed into a small row of neat dwelling-houses, and thus occupied for some years—when the big Brooklyn fire occurred in 1848, and destroyed that row amongst much other property.

No theatre was established in Brooklyn, after this failure, till the sometime popular Brooklyn Museum was put up at the corner of Orange and Fulton streets, a few years ago, by Mr. John E. Cammeyer. It is but justice to say that while they lasted the performances of this second Thespian establishment were of a very excellent character, being all in the range of "the legitimate drama." The company was really a good one, though small; and two or three of the performers were of superior talent and national reputation. The attendence, for a while, was up to the paying point, and at one time, it was thought we were going to have the theatre as "a permanency" in our city. But by degrees the fickle favor of the public cooled; the audiences declined—New York perhaps offered greater inducements—and the consequence was, Manager Lovell and his talented wife had to shut up shop.

Since then, nothing has occurred till the establishment of our noble Academy—which has already commenced giving regular stage performances.

What did we have, for our amusements, previous to these theatres, and during the blanks, generally long drawn out, when they held not their revels? Well, a variety of ways of passing the time presented themselves that would now be voted decidedly slow, but "did" for the Brooklyn of those days. There were the churches, especially the Methodist ones, with their frequent "revivals." These last occurrences drew out all the young fellows, who attended with demure faces but always on the watch for deviltry. Then we had various sorts of "celebrations"—sometimes of the Sunday Schools, sometimes the regular educational establishments, sometimes of an anniversary of one kind or another. Of course we came out great on a Fourth of July celebration. This was always an affair to be carefully seen to and planned deliberately—and the "oration" was something talked of both beforehand and long afterward. Great were the jealousies and heartburnings among the young lawyers over the preference and selection to this important post, namely, that of orator to the annual Fourth of July celebration. It created as much buzz and electioneering by-play, on a small scale, as among the cardinals in Rome, when the Pope's chair is vacant, the choice for his successor. Next to the orator was the lucky individual who should be selected to "read the Declaration of Independence." Next again to him was the "Grand Marshal," of whose responsibilities, and the dignity of whose position, words are hardly immense enough to make out the statement.

Sometimes there was quite a godsend. Some distinguished person, for instance, would visit New York, and then it would go hard with us if we did not get him over to Brooklyn. Perhaps it would be the President of the United States. Once it was no less a personage than the great and good Lafayette. This was on the Fourth of July, 1825. The writer of these veracious penjottings remembers the whole occasion and scene with perfect distinctness, although he was then only a little boy in his seventh year.

The day was a very pleasant one. The whole village, with all its population, old and young, gentle and simple, turned out en-masse. The principal regular feature of the show was (for want of any military), the marshalling into two parallel lines, with a space of twenty feet between them, of all the boys and girls of Brooklyn. These two lines, facing inward, made a lane, through which Lafayette rode slowly in a carriage. It was an old-fashioned yellow coach; and, indeed, the whole proceeding was of an ancient primitive kind, very staid, without any cheering, but then a plentiful waving of white pocket handkerchiefs from the ladies. The two lines of boys and girls ranged from Fulton Ferry landing along up to Henry Street. As our readers will understand, it was something very different from such a turnout of modern date, as that which welcomed the Prince of Wales or the Japanese Ambassadors, or President Lincoln last spring. Still, as near as we can remember, it must have had an air of simplicity, naturalness and freedom from ostentation or clap-trap—and was not without a smack of antique grandeur too. For there were quite a number of "old Revolutionaries" on the ground, and along the line of march; and their bent forms and white hair gave a picturesque contrast to the blooming faces of the boys and girls to be seen in all directions in such numbers. The sentiment of the occasion, moreover, made up in quality and in solemnity what was wanting in spangles, epaulettes, policemen, and brass bands—not the first sign of any of which graced the occasion.

Lafayette rode to the corner of Cranberry and Henry streets, where he laid the corner stone of the Apprentices Library Building (now superseded by the Brooklyn Armory). From there he was driven a pleasant route along the Heights (Clover Hill), and so to a collation, if we remember rightly to the Military Garden.

We shall have something further to say of this visit of Lafayette in a future article, giving a history of the old Apprentices Library.

Such were some of the "events" of those former times in

Brooklyn. There were not wanting, during the winter nights for any who enjoyed them, livelier "frolics," balls, sleigh rides (we had good sleighing almost every winter then), parties, lectures, concerts, and various itinerant shows; to say nothing of the always popular "singing school"—now quite among the things that were, but are not.

Upon the whole, we guess people, old and young, of six or seven lustrums gone, had just as good a time without our more modern excitements and amusements as we do now with them.

IX

RELIGIOUS RECORD OF BROOKLYN

FIRST MINISTER OF THE COLONY

FORM OF DOCTRINE

HERETICS

QUAKERS TREATED WITH SEVERITY

FIRST CHURCH IN KINGS COUNTY,
AT FLATBUSH

POPULATION OF BROOKLYN IN 1660

A CHURCH IN BROOKLYN, 1666

DESCRIPTION AND HISTORY OF THIS
CHURCH AND ITS LOCALITY

CLASSIS OF AMSTERDAM

NEW CHURCH OF 1807

ANOTHER IN 1834, WHICH IS THE
PRESENT ONE

INDIAN PREACHERS IN LONG ISLAND

SAMSON OCCOM

The religious growth and character of a settlement is by no means the least important part of its record. We will, in this paper, present the statement of some of the first beginnings and subsequent continuations of "the church," especially of one venerable edifice, before alluded to, that stood in Brooklyn for over a hundred years.

The first regularly ordained minister in the settlement of the New Netherlands was the Reverend Everard Bogardus, who was brought over with Governor Van Twiller, in 1629. Previous to his arrival (and, indeed, for some time afterward), as there was no church built, the congregation carried on their exercises in a barn, said to have been situated at the corner of Broad and Stone streets, in New York. We have, however, authentic records of the Reformed Dutch Church in the colony only back to the date of 1639.

It will be remembered that the English settlers were interspersed with the Dutch, almost from the very beginning. But there was little or no difference of belief. The doctrine generally taught was from the confession of faith adopted by the Assembly of Divines at Westminister in 1642. The congregational form of church government prevailed till the year 1747, when the Presbyterian order was chosen as better adapted to preserve the purity of doctrine. Indeed, from the first, the organization of churches, under authority, in the Dutch settlements here (as among the Puritans to the east), was considered one of the earliest things to be attended to.

During the Dutch administration, and partially during the English afterward, the governors claimed the sole right of licensing preachers, which was generally acquiesced in as necessary to keep out interlopers and promulgers of false doctrine. Some of these were occasionally treated with severity. During the administration of Governor Stuyvesant, a very respectable member of the Quaker faith was arrested, imprisoned a while, and then transported in the next ship to

Holland, as a dangerous heretic. Another was confined in the jail in Queens County for over a year. It will be remembered, however, that the Quakers, for a while after the sect originated, were the subject of general persecution and prejudice. In New England they were even condemned to death.

No doubt, according to what has been intimated, the settlers instituted religious meetings of an informal character from the very first. But, for some years, those who desired to attend the ministrations of a regularly ordained clergyman, on the Sabbath, had to cross the river to Manhattan Island. There Dominie Bogardus continued his ministrations till 1647, when he was succeeded by Dominie Johannus Backerus, who continued only a couple of years—and he by others, etc.—down to 1654.

Until the latter date there had been no regularly ordained clergyman, with a church to preach in, in Brooklyn. It is necessary to state, also, that the Brooklyn of that period did not cluster toward the great ferries as now, but was situated about a mile inland. All these, and also the inhabitants of Midwout (Flatbush) and Amersfort (Flatlands) had to make the journey, on the Sabbath, over to Manhattan Island, to "go to church."

In 1654, Dominie Johannes Theodorus Polhemus landed here, from a visit to South America, and was invited by the settlers in Kings County to stop and preach for them. Upon his acceptance of the call, and the governor granting the requisite license, a church was built (this was at Flatbush), in the form of a cross, sixty feet the longest way, and twenty-eight the other. It was built by general subscription of all the settlements; and here Dominie Polhemus was duly installed. This may be called the first formal establishment of religion in our settlement. It was the Presbyterian church, of the form above alluded to.

Dominie Polhemus preached every Sunday morning in this new cruciform church, and in the afternoons alternately in Brooklyn (toward the ferry), and at Flatlands. In this condition things remained for six years.

Brooklyn proper had by this time increased to thirty-one families, comprising one hundred and thirty-four souls. In the year last mentioned it is recorded that there were twenty-four specific Brooklyn members of the Flatbush congregation, with one elder, and two deacons.

This induced the Brooklynites to set up for themselves, and in 1660, they offered a call to Dominie Selyns, which he accepted; and from that date it was unnecessary to go either to Manhattan Island or Flatbush, on the Sabbath.

For a while, the Brooklyn congregation (like the beginning at New York) worshipped in a barn. But the attendance was regular and full, and had many accessions from Flatbush, Gravesend, and from New Amsterdam, across the river. So that but a short time passed before it was determined to build an eligible church.

This was done in 1666. In a former paper we have described this first Brooklyn church, and given some items of its history. For it had quite a history. It stood for over a century—indeed for some hundred and twenty-five or thirty years, and for the greater part of that time was the only church in Brooklyn. It stood on what is now Fulton Avenue, near Duffield Street, right in the middle of the road, which passed by it on either side. It was either a round, or octagonal shaped building, and had a conical roof. Some accounts say that it was pulled down in 1791; but an aged Brooklynite, yet living, who came here in the year 1800, tells the writer of these sketches that it was not destroyed till some few years after he came to Brooklyn.

This edifice, however, was, as we said, the beginning of the church in Brooklyn. It was the only religious edifice here at the outset of the Revolutionary War. And though, in 1664, the Dutch power in the New Netherlands was yielded up to the British, it was expressly stipulated by the old authorities that the existing forms of worship, and full liberty of conscience and of church discipline, were to be reserved to the inhabitants.

The Classis of Amsterdam, which had been from the first the ecclesiastical superior of all the Dutch churches in the New Netherlands, continued to be so over them all, until 1772, when the American Reformed Dutch Church became independent of all foreign authority, yet continued in friendly correspondence with the mother church, for a long while afterward.

The Reformed Dutch Church, which held this edifice, and formed its congregation, determined, soon after the commencement of the present century, on a new and larger building. The location was changed, and placed where it now is (in Joralemon Street, south of the City Hall). Here, in December, 1807, a large new church of dark grey stone was opened for public worship—and here it stood, like the oldest son of the patriarch that had preceded it, till 1834. At that time, it had become both too small and too old-fashioned, and the consistory determined on still a newer and handsomer building. The result of their determination was the present edifice (which is copied from the architecture of the celebrated Parthenon, the temple of Minerva at Athens). It is a handsome edifice; but a comparison, in thought, between it and the old round thatch-roofed church that stood in the middle of the road excites some curious reflections.

Many of our readers will doubtless be interested in knowing that Long Island, in the earlier times (during the 18th century), furnished several Indian preachers, of good Christian repute. The records of the Presbyterian churches of the island contain accounts of several such preachers. One in particular, named Samson Occom, was quite celebrated, having gone abroad and preached in London, it is said before the King and Queen. This Samson was born in 1723, and was thoroughly educated by a New England minister. In 1755 he established a school and church for Indians on the east end of the island. He was regularly ordained, and occasionally travelled to the main land—sometimes visiting Brooklyn and New York, and preaching. It was in 1767 that he visited England. While there he preached in Whitefield's church.

Here on Long Island, to the Indians, he preached in their own dialect—and accounts say that he was a free, strong and graceful orator.

X

The old graveyards of Brooklyn! What a history is contained in them! Not so much, to be sure, that comes home to the vast proportion of the present two hundred and seventy-five thousand of our inhabitants who have planted themselves among us for the last thirty years—or mostly, indeed, within the last ten years. Not so much to them, we say. But much, ever so much, to all the descendants of the old stock. Much also, in connection with the name of our city, and with its settlement, growth, associations, and with crowds of interesting traditions and venerable facts of our city—giving it a broad mellow light, a retrospective and antiquarian background. Much that, as they read these lines (as we hope and trust they may, for such things are among the pensive pleasures of advanced age), will bring up, by their perusal, to the memory of those who are left of every Brooklyn born and Brooklyn raised man and woman, thoughts of other days—of the days of youth, the pleasures, the friends, scenes and persons long faded away—the appearance of Brooklyn when it was a scattered, rural village of a few hundred people. We are at once carried back to the commencement of the present century—to the "last war"— the village charters—the cutting through and paving of the principal thoroughfares—the digging away of hills—the city charter—and a hundred other of the precedents and preparations which have so rapidly been gone through within the last thirty years, and left for signs of themselves the present advanced condition of this noble, wealthy, intelligent, cultivated, populous, and every way remarkable and to be proud of Brooklyn of ours.

But if we run on in this way we shall gossip up all the time we had devoted, between ourselves and you, gentle reader (we like the old phrase yet), to a few remarks on one or two of the old graveyards of Brooklyn. We dare say that it is even necessary to say in advance, to a great many

77

of the present inhabitants, that there actually *are* several such old burial places, yet traceable, in our midst.

One of the oldest and roomiest burial-grounds in Brooklyn was that in Fulton Avenue, just above Smith Street. This was the depository of the dead appertaining to the old Dutch church that stood at the commencement of the present century on a location upon the turnpike road, now Fulton Avenue, just above Duffield Street. (This is about as near as we can get at it. We have never seen the old meeting-house, known in history as "the Brooklyn church," but there are persons yet living in Brooklyn who have, and can point out the spot, as they have pointed it out accurately to us.) That was a real old Dutch church. It stood right in the middle of the highway, which passed up and down both sides of it. It was a round building or octagon, and had a high conical roof; we think we have been told it was thatched, but we are not certain. This church was dismantled and removed early in the present century—somewhere about the year 1803–8, or perhaps previously. In its stead a massive, square, dark-grey, old-fashioned stone church was built, the location being changed to Joralemon Street. The site of this grey stone was the same one now occupied by the Dutch Reformed Church in the rear of the City Hall. We have been in that grey stone church often—went to Sunday School there. It was torn down and gave place to the present building some twenty or twenty-five years ago.

As to burial deposits, contemporary with the historical old Dutch church first mentioned, the said burial deposits were often made, in aboriginal times, irrespective of any regular ground, specifically belonging to any church. Families here, in those times, had their own burial places. On the farms around Brooklyn, and on ground that is now *in* Brooklyn, far inside of its outer wards, it was not uncommon, half a generation ago to frequently see these last rest-ing-spots of the passed-away of the original families of this end of the island. We have frequently seen them when a youngster while rambling about this part of Kings County. We recollect one small one, in particular, containing four or five graves, close along Fulton Avenue, nearly opposite the residence of Samuel Fleet, Esq. This, no doubt, used to appertain to the old round church, destroyed fifty years ago. The graves were surrounded with a fence of open woodwork, and remained there down to the grading and paving of Fulton Avenue, a few years since.

All these fractional burying-spots, in old Brooklyn, although it would be of interest to trace them, and point out the spots, they are now so long obliterated, covered with houses and stores, and the families whose progenitors they hold broken up, that it is next to impossible.

A few families or persons of distinction had vaults belonging to, or under the pavement of, the old historical Brooklyn church. Andrew Demarest, a very aged citizen, now living, was present at the demolition of this church, mentioned as early in the present century. We remember Mr. Demarest, in a talk we once had with him on the subject of the dismantling of this church, telling us the following among the other incidents connected with it. In removing the traces of the church, the workmen came upon a dead body buried there, dressed in the complete uniform of a British officer of rank. The body was in remarkable preservation, in the midst of its showy uniform, buttons, epaulettes, gold lace, cocked hat, sword by its side, etc. It was exhumed one pleasant morning, soon after the men commenced working; and the event making a good deal of talk, before noon a large part of the inhabitants of Brooklyn had collected to take a look at the body before it was removed. Among the rest, it happened there came a lady who distinctly remembered the burial of the officer, many years before. She did not know the name, as she was a little girl when it happened. It was of a British officer killed at the Battle of Brooklyn in 1776, and buried there a couple of days afterward, when the royal troops took possession, after Washington retreated. We think Mr. Demarest told us the lady was one of the Duffield family. What a vivid picture the whole occurrence serves to bring up before us!

The church we mention, besides its being a sort of central point of old Brooklyn graves, has, in the reminiscences of it, many high and serious historical associations. Washington made it his headquarters during the day and night of his famous retreat after the battle just alluded to. It has much that is worth recording, in connection with that momentous occurrence (the pivot, as it was, of our Revolutionary War), and of some other matters still; but for our present purposes we can only consider it in connection with the subject named at the head of our article. We must, indeed, keep more closely to our theme.

In the now obliterated burial place in Fulton Avenue, above Smith Street, were, but a few seasons since, to be found members of all the old families of this end of the island—from the settlers that came hither from Holland—indeed, the suggestions of a complete history of our city, from the beginning down to the late date when burials in our limits were prohibited by law. What material for reflection in that old place of graves! From it, and also the graveyard in Fulton Street, opposite the Globe Hotel (of which more anon), might be made out from the solemn installments there, during the times by-gone, nearly all that relates to the personal history of our city, and, by consequence, suggesting the whole of its material history and progress.

The old graveyards, we say, would tell it all, from the beginning. Many a family tree—many a once familiar name would be resumed—and, indeed, many a yet familiar Brook-

WALT WHITMAN. A picture taken in the early 1850's.

THE NEW YORK SKYLINE IN THE EARLY 1850's. A view of lower Manhattan, as seen from the East River.

(Courtesy The Bettmann Archive)

CASTLE GARDEN, 1852. The site of many cultural and civic events attended by Whitman and his contemporaries.

(Courtesy The Bettmann Archive)

DOWNTOWN BROOKLYN IN THE LATE 1860's. A view of Fulton Street, as seen from the ferry landing.

(Courtesy The Bettmann Archive)

FORTY-SECOND STREET, 1855. This view, looking southward, shows the Croton Reservoir and the Crystal Palace in the foreground, facing Forty-Second Street. Fifth Avenue is at the left foreground, by the Reservoir.

(Courtesy The Bettmann Archive)

THE FERRY. A ferryboat crossing from Manhattan to Brooklyn in the 1840's.

(Courtesy The Bettmann Archive)

DOWNTOWN BROOKLYN IN THE LATE 1810's. A reproduction of the painting, "Guy's Snow Scene," discussed by Whitman.

(Courtesy The Bettmann Archive)

THE FULTON FERRY LANDING. The Manhattan terminal of the Fulton Ferry in the early 1860's.

(Courtesy The Bettmann Archive)

THE BROOKLYN SKYLINE IN THE LATE 1840's. As seen from lower Manhattan.

(Courtesy The Bettmann Archive)

BROOKLYN HEIGHTS, ABOUT 1850. A view of Montague Street, showing Lover's Promenade.

(Courtesy The Bettmann Archive)

PARK ROW IN THE LATE 1840's. A view of the Park Row stores in lower Manhattan.

(Courtesy The Bettmann Archive)

NEW YORK AND BROOKLYN IN THE EARLY 1850's. A panoramic view looking northward from New York Bay.

(Courtesy The Bettmann Archive)

BROADWAY IN 1850. The heart of Manhattan in Whitman's day. At left is Barnum's Museum, while on the opposite side are Brady's Daguerreotype Gallery, then St. Paul's Chapel, and on the extreme right, the fashionable Astor House, gathering place of New York society and literati.

(Courtesy The Bettmann Archive)

lyn name too. The main trunks perhaps are there; at any rate, many of the branches, near and remote, are there. By blood, by marriage, by some or another tie, thousands are yet connected there in those old graveyards—soon every trace of them, however, to be utterly rubbed out, and strangers busy buying and selling on the location of those memorable grounds.

There are (even while we write it is necessary to substitute *were*) the names of Bergen, Hegeman, Vandewater, Johnson, Garretson, Lefferts, Rapelye, Remsen, Vechte, Boerum, Duffield, Suydam, Doughty, Polhemus, Furman, Mercein, Stanton, Clarke, Joralemon, Moser, Vanderveer, Barkeloo, Sprague, Waring, Rushmore, Pierrepont, Van Nostrand, Leavitt, Walton, Bache, Thorne, Hicks, Prince, Van Wagener, Skillman, Romaine and Willoughby, and many other well-established Brooklyn families besides, in those old collections, the memory of equally important ones escaping us. It is an almost awful thought that, with all the wealth of many of those grand and powerful families above-named, the ones who have originated and belonged to them, and all the possessions of their descendants, have not been permitted to hold uncontested "the measure of their own graves."

We have alluded to the old graveyard in Fulton Street, opposite the Globe Hotel. The work of removing the remains deposited here (including not a few of those whose family appellations are given above), has been steadily going on for some months behind that tall placarded fence. In three months from now a row of magnificent stores will uprise and be completed on this ground; and then but a few years more and the recollection of the former sacredness of the spot will have entirely passed away. Gorgeous with rich goods, seen through plate glass windows, and splendid with glittering jets of gas at night, and resonant with the hum of the voices of crowds, is, or will be, the spot. A fit illustration of the rapid changes of this kaleidoscope of alteration and death we call life.

Before we pass to another topic, we must give of this yet visible graveyard an episode that comes within our own knowledge. It is of an occurrence that happened in 1829, of a beautiful June day, namely, of the steam-frigate *Fulton* (the first steam vessel ever built for any government) being blown up by the vengeance of an exasperated sailor who fired the powder magazine, and caused the death of between forty and fifty persons. The writer of these paragraphs, then a boy of just ten years old, was at the public school, corner of Adams and Concord Street. We remember the dull shock that was felt in the building as of something like an earthquake—for the vessel was moored at the Navy Yard. But more distinctly do we remember, two or three days afterwards, the funeral of one of the officers in the graveyard above mentioned. It was a full military and naval funeral—the sailors marching two by two, hand in hand, banners tied up and bound in black crape, the muffled drums beating, the bugles wailing forth the mournful peals of a dead march. We remember it all—remember following the procession, boy-like, from beginning to end. We remember the soldiers firing the salute over the grave. And then how everything changed with the dashing and merry jig played by the same bugles and drums, as they made their exit from the graveyard and wended rapidly home.

The subject we have opened upon has a volume contained within it;—yet one more passing mention and we have done. A late paper alludes to the dead of the old prison ships— yet we must return to the subject again. Deficient would that article be on Brooklyn burial places—lacking one of its most vital points, that did not record, before it yet entirely rots away, the existence among us of a strange, rickety, mildewed, tumble-down wooden structure on Hudson Avenue (Jackson Street), a short half mile above the ferry, with its walls covered by a now almost illegible inscription. This wretched piece of wood-work, (it would not bring three dollars to-day if put up at auction), is all that in a monumental form tells of the proudest and most precious legacy our city holds, from the past, to pass onward to the patriotism of the future. We allude to the remains, deposited in Brooklyn soil, adjacent to the Wallabout, of those twelve thousand unnamed Revolutionary patriots, "roughs," who were from time to time taken in battle by the British, and incarcerated in the celebrated prison ships. These remains are from all the original Thirteen States—who, from 1776 to 1783, died of sickness, starvation, or cruelty, and were, from day to day, brought ashore and dumped in the sand, in careless heaps, uncoffined, uncared for, with just enough dirt thrown over them to prevent the neighboring air from becoming pestilential.

Most of the unknown patriots' remains, of course, are now altogether lost, built over, dug away, etc., and scattered to the elements. But they were strewed so plenteously that a fair portion has been secured and kept. The wooden structure above alluded to was put up to memorize a great and expensive display in 1808, when a portion of the dead relics of the martyrs of the prison ships were, as narrated by us the other day, carried through the streets of New York and Brooklyn in a procession, and deposited here—and the aforesaid wooden mausoleum temporarily erected, to mark the spot, by the Tammany Society of New York. It is now an instructive sight. We advise the reader to go visit it. It is probably the most slatternly and dirtiest object to be seen anywhere in Brooklyn. Likewise it has a valuable moral.

XI

We must not omit, in hastily penning these gossiping chronicles, to make brief mention of some of the localities of Brooklyn, now occupied by public buildings, parks, or rows of elegant private dwellings—alluding to them as they appeared thirty years ago. Carrying our statement farther back, from the words of those who knew them previously, we will also give a few paragraphs of "the last war," and matters of that ilk.

The military reputation which of right belongs to Brooklyn does not cluster merely around our present companies of well-drilled soldiers, nor on what appertains to the Brooklyn Armory in Henry Street, or the Arsenal on Portland Avenue. Yet the latter is more than usually appropriate for a building for military purposes for our city; for it was in this very neighborhood that the lines of fortified posts and entrenchments were made, reaching from Wallabout to Red Hook, that formed the American lines, in the Battle of Long Island, in the early part of the Revolutionary War. It was this line of rude fortifications that stopped the progress of the enemy, and secured the safety of the American troops—till Washington made his masterly retreat over to New York Island, which saved the Revolutionary cause.

On the same neighborhood were thrown the hasty entrenchments during the last war—the men and boys of New York and Brooklyn turned out voluntarily with "pickaxes, shovels and spade" (as the song hath it) to provide for any emergency that might happen. For several days there were large forces of such volunteers at work, under officers appointed to oversee them—one force duly relieving another. It was feared that the British fleet might make an attempt to land, and cross the river in the same way as in 1776—and the fortified embankments were intended to oppose them. If the reader is curious in the matter, he will find, here and there, an old Brooklynite left (and not a few New Yorkers

87

also), who took a hand in the dirt-digging and throwing up
the embankments of the occasion. The women, as usual, ever
forward in good works, assisted by gifts of food, drink, etc.,
and often enlivened the scene with their presence. Happily,
however, the last war passed over without any war-guns having occasion to be fired on these particular shores of ours—
the most of that business, as it turned out, transpiring not
on land, but on the sea, where America first learned that
aboard ship she was as good as the best of 'em.

The above mentioned trenches and embankments, which
many of our readers will remember as existing a very few
years ago, on the sight of the present Washington Park
(Fort Greene), were therefore not, as many supposed,
relics of its Revolutionary experience of '76 but of the attempt, just described, to prepare to meet the enemy during
the war of 1812, '13, should they seek to land here.

These trenches and embankments, made in 1812, remained, indeed, in pretty much the same condition down to
the commencement of the improvement for Washington
Park. Some of the highest walls of the present park are
literally the ground thrown up by the patriotic hands of the
men and boy volunteers we have spoken of—those banks
being very properly left as they were, and included in the
plan of the park.

Then the old powder-houses that dotted this section of
our city in days of yore. Will there not be some of our readers who will recollect those old weird-looking, unshaded,
unfenced powder-houses? One of them stood in immediate
proximity to the site of the present Arsenal, if not on the
exact spot. These powder-houses were covered with slate,
and were the only edifices in the neighborhood—being placed
out there, at a safe distance from the thickly settled parts
of the city (or rather village, as it then was), which were
around the Old and New Ferries, and up, perhaps, as high

as Cranberry or Concord streets. The whole scene, around the grounds of the present Arsenal was, indeed, in those days, a wild hilly, unfenced, open landscape—something far different from its present appearance. It was quite a place for parties of men and boys for a Sunday or holiday jaunt from New York, and offered almost as desert and bleak an appearance as the untenanted wilds on the east end of Long Island do at this day.

No part of the city has made a more utter revolution in its topography than this quarter of Brooklyn. All the old landmarks, roads, edifices, etc., are obliterated. The only one we noticed standing, in a tour of observation we made not long since, was the old Dutch house, or rather the ruins of it, on the estate of the late venerable Jeremiah Johnson—and formerly, we believe, his own residence. This was on Kent Avenue, and nigh the present residence of his son Barnet Johnson. But we believe even the ruins of that old building are now obliterated.

Then the old Potter's Field. During the war times, and down to about twelve or fifteen years ago, the ground on which the present Arsenal is built, and for some distance west of it (about two acres in the blocks between Myrtle and Park avenues and now partly intersected by Hampden Avenue), were appropriated to a free city burial yard, or Potter's Field. Many hundreds of people were buried there, and the workmen engaged in excavating for cellars, etc., in that neighborhood, continually come, at the present day, upon the remains of those burials.

In the same neighborhood stood the county Alms House (the house is yet standing). Then the buildings and grounds (which yet belong to the city) were leased to the Government for Marine barracks. It is the old yellow wooden shanty on Park Avenue, near Raymond Street, now all dismantled.

Then the present City Park, at the Wallabout. Very different from its contemporary appearance, with pleasant grass and clover patches, in summer, and shaded with trees, was its appearance when the middle-aged men of the present day were young fellows. All about there used to be a vast, low, miry, stagnant place, covered with a shallow depth of water, on which, in summer, was spread a sickening yellow scum. Only one or two roads, and a bridge, made this bad spread of a place passable. Part of it was, in due time, filled up by the city, and forms the present City Park, with its northerly front on Flushing Avenue. The rest has been, by degrees, filled up by its owners—until the stagnant ponds and black creeks where the little Brooklyn boys of twenty-six or seven years ago used to go Saturday afternoons and catch "killy-fish" with a bent pin and a piece of tow string have altogether disappeared, and left no sign or memento, except in such reminiscences as those of ours.

Perhaps one of the facts which will prove the tremendous *advancement* we have made, and the difference between that era and the present, will be a little bit of the financial exhibit of the Brooklyn of the time. Here, then, is the budget of our city for 1831—and you can see, reader, what strides we have made in exactly thirty years! It is the sum estimated, raised, and laid out for the expenses of Brooklyn for the then current year:

BROOKLYN EXPENSES, 1831

Police (of those days)	$3,000
Fire Department	1,400
Salaries of officers	1,200 !
Interest on Brooklyn debt	600
Water, Pumps, Cisterns, &c.	1,200
Contingent expenses	2,600 !
Grand Total	$10,000 ! !

Which, we think, will be considered very moderate—and especially instructive, in comparison with *these* days. It must be stated, however, that the above sum was the utmost limit of the moneys allowed by law of the Legislature to be raised out of the good people of Brooklyn through the tax-gatherers. Perhaps it would be worth while to try a limit to tax-gathering again—but we suppose we would have to extend the sum a little beyond the "grand total" afore specified.

XII

OUR COUNTY JAIL

THE OLD EDIFICE AT FLATBUSH—
BURNED DOWN EIGHTY YEARS AGO

COURTS CHANGED TO APPRENTICES
LIBRARY, BROOKLYN

THE ACT OF 1835

HALL'S EXCHANGE BUILDING

NEW COURT HOUSE TROUBLES

THE ROMANCE OF A JAIL BUILDING

We don't know what school or name of architecture our well-known Kings County Jail and Court House in Raymond Street would come under; but it very well answers, and has answered, the purposes for which it was built—namely, as the place of incarceration for prisoners, and afterwards a place of meeting for the County Courts and Board of Supervisors, and for a residence for the Sheriff, etc.

The old Jail and Court House for the people of Brooklyn (said people comprising, of course, the main portion of the County of Kings), as is probably known to many of our readers, used to be at Flatbush, and the County Courts were, until a comparatively late period, required by law to be held there—making it incumbent on our Brooklyn and New York lawyers, with all their witnesses, etc., to pack out there, and, after submitting to the "law's delay," sometimes to their great inconvenience, await the slow or rapid progress of their trials, and then come home again, perhaps to return the next day, and again the next.

About the year 1826, we believe, a law was procured to be passed by the Legislature that thenceforward the Courts of Common Pleas and General Sessions of the Peace should be held "alternately at the Court-house at Flatbush, and at the Apprentices Library in the city of Brooklyn." Soon after this, things advanced still farther toward a complete change of locality. In 1829 or '30 a law was passed empowering the Board of Supervisors to raise, by tax, a sum of money, to devote the same to "the purchase of lots of land in the village of Brooklyn, and erecting a suitable building thereon, for the accommodation of the courts of the said county, when the same, or any of them, may be held in the said village of Brooklyn." The carrying out of the requirements of this law, however, was delayed, and finally negatived by the influence of Flatbush property owners, etc.

We think it was about the year 1832 the old Jail and
Court House at Flatbush caught fire and was burned down
(Dec. 1st, 1832). So that the next year another law was
passed, to the effect that "a Court-house and Jail in and for
the county of Kings shall be erected in the village of Brooklyn"; and under this enactment three commissioners were
appointed to purchase an appropriate and central site for
the building. When the Court House should be so far completed as to be prepared for the public convenience, a cer-
tificate to that effect should be procured from the first judge
of the county, and thereafter all the terms of the Court of
Common Pleas and General Sessions of the Peace were to
be held, and all writs and processes were returnable, at the
new Court House in Brooklyn. In the meantime, as the
Flatbush edifice was destroyed, the terms of the county
courts that were to have been held at that place were trans-
ferred to the Apprentices Library in Brooklyn. Of course
our readers are aware that this edifice was formely on the
site of the present City Armory in Henry Street.

Soon after the fire at Flatbush, the present jail in Raymond Street was authorized and built—as it was impera-
tively necessary of course that there should be some place
for the safe keeping of criminals. Still, however, the project
of a specific Court House hung fire; for we believe that all
along, during the period of the years 1835, to '40, '42, etc.,
the actual Court House of the county was the Apprentices
Library building just alluded to, and that there the judicial
proceedings were held, notices posted, etc. There seems to
have been a good deal of acrimonious feeling mixed up in
the business. The people of Flatbush thought that they had
a prescriptive right to the locality there of the county Jail
and Court House, pretty much in the same way that the
folks of Philadelphia think that they have a right to the
United States Mint, because it has been there a long while.

Then there were conflicting opinions too about the preference for different sites. We jot these particulars and details,
however, more to put the matter on record than because it
is of very great importance.

The building commenced as Court House in addition
to its legitimate purpose as jail about sixteen or seven-
teen years ago—under authority of an act of the Legislature passed in 1835. As there has been considerable dis-
cussion about this act we will give an account of it. By this
act, passed in 1835, the Judges and Supervisors of the
County of Kings, whenever they should deem "the present
Court Room in the Apprentices Library" unsafe or incon-
venient for the purpose of holding courts therein, were
authorized, from time to time, to designate such other place
in the City of Brooklyn as they should think proper; whereupon a rule of the court should be made for that purpose,
"and such other place shall become from that time for all
legal purposes the Court House of the said county until a
new Court House shall be completed. But nothing herein
contained shall be construed to invalidate notices posted at
the Apprentices Library, or any other place in the designated as aforesaid, previous to such rule of the Court for
changing the place of holding Courts being made." By the
eighth section of this act, the Board of Supervisors was
authorized to sell "the lot of land on which the Court House
and Jail at Flatbush, lately destroyed by fire, was situated."

In pursuance of this act, the judges and supervisors, in
March 1845, designated the County Jail in Raymond Street
as the place of holding the courts of the county. The resolution adopted on that occasion recites that a room in Hall's
Exchange Building had therefore been legally designated as
aforesaid, and was then used for holding courts in the
county. This Exchange building was quite a large edifice at
the corner of Fulton and Cranberry streets, and the third

story was for some time used as a place of meeting for the Common Council.

Things continued in abeyance till 1853, when we find a legislative act that "the Board of Supervisors of the County of Kings are hereby authorized to borrow a sum not exceeding one hundred thousand dollars, and to expend the same in the purchase of a site and erection of a building for the accommodation of such of the county officers of said county as said Board of Supervisors shall determine." By the second and third sections the County Treasurer was authorized under the direction of the Board to borrow on the credit of the county the whole or a portion of the sum as the Board might determine, and give his official bond or bonds for the payment of the same with interest; and the Board was directed "to levy and collect such sums annually as should be sufficient to pay the interest on the loan, and to reimburse the principal in annual instalments as they should become payable."

Under this enactment, there has since been kept up a succession of turmoils and passages and repeals of resolutions, the history of which is as long as the Trojan War. Half a dozen different sites have been fixed upon. Some of these, we believe, were really purchased; and the Supreme Court and Court of Appeals were invoked to settle the conflicting claims of the different parties. The end of all has happily been the selection for a new Court House of the site at the commencement of Fulton Avenue, near the City Hall, where the building is now in progress.

Of course, in connection with the history of the jail there is a long and varied interior history, full of interest and indeed of romance.

An account of the different sheriffs' administrations, and of the residence of many of them and their families in the dwelling part of the jail, would alone be full of points of attraction to a large class of citizens of Brooklyn. The administration some years since of Sheriff Daniel Van Voorhies, that of Sheriff Lott, the late administration of Sheriff Remsen, and the rule of the present deservedly popular and judicious Sheriff Campbell, might all come in for a share of such an abstract.

A detailed account of the internal and personal scenes and sights of the jail, with cases of marked interest among the prisoners, and an idea of the method of securing, feeding and general treatment of the prisoners, we propose to make before long, through a visit and personal inspection of affairs at the jail.

XIII

ORIGINAL NAME OF THIS ISLAND

PAUMANOK

SHALL IT BE RESUMED?

FUTURE CONSIDERATIONS

ONE REMINISCENCE OF THE RED MEN,
AT LEAST, OUGHT TO BE PRESERVED
HERE, IN THEIR OWN TONGUE.

TERRITORIAL STATISTICS OF
LONG ISLAND

LENGTH, BREADTH, AND AREA

ITS SMALL ISLANDS ADJOINING

FUTURE POPULATION

STATE OF PAUMANOK

LANDED INTEREST VALUED

SOUTH BAY

We have heard it suggested (and we think the idea worth serious consideration), that the original name of this island ought on many accounts to be resumed, and made the legal and customary name again. That original name was PAU-MANOK, the sense of which is, or has been traced to be, as we have heard, "the island with its breast long drawn out, and laid against the sea." This is a beautiful and appropriate signification, as the word itself is a pleasant one to the ear.

It is argued that there are some dozen or twenty Long Islands here and there on the American coast and in the Great Lakes, and that this important territory ought to have something by which it could be specially known; something belonging to itself, which would by time and association become a source of pride and convey the idea of home. It is perhaps best not to change the settled name of a place on frivolous or sentimental reasons; but as the region we are speaking of is going to be made in future times significant as the seat of one of the most beautiful and intelligent of the first class cities of the world (namely, this Brooklyn of ours), we do not know but we would seriously favor a project for giving us back again, for the island on which it stands, the name of *Paumanok*.

The word occurs in all the aboriginal deeds, and was used by the first Dutch settlers, in speaking or writing of the territory here. It was then spelt in various ways, according to the custom which, until a comparatively modern date, did not acquire or indeed allow a uniform standard of orthography, even in some of the commonest every day words. Some of the old deeds spell it *Paumanake*.

By the allusions of the Dutch and English settlers, and from old ecclesiastical records (to which all historical memoirs are so much indebted), we gather also that there were several other terms by which the island was designated. It was sometimes called *Sewant-hackey* (the place of the shells), and also *Mattowak* or *Mattawake*. The name of Long Island was given to it by the English at or soon after the period of their finally taking the government.

So upon the whole we think it might be not only a verbal, but a utilitarian, piece of improvement to restore the old name of the island. It would be a kind of poetic justice to the departed tribes of the great nation of the Lenni-Lenape, or Delawares, of which stock the aborigines of this region were a part. Their language has been pronounced by the etymologists to be the most advanced and regular of all the Indian dialects; and both in natural intelligence and in courage they were up to the highest standard known here when the Europeans first landed. Now that they have all forever departed, it seems as if their shades deserve at least the poor recompense of the compliment connected in preserving the old name by which they themselves designated and knew this territory.

But while we are discussing the choice of the best nomenclature for what now passes as Long Island, there will be a very great portion of our readers who have by no means very definite notions of the important physical facts of the island itself. We will therefore devote this and the following paper to an abstract of such information. It will be found of interest, for we do not believe there is an equal extent of territory anywhere which has superior points of advantage in some of the first respects that make a country notable and interesting. In salubrity, Brooklyn is eminent, as has long been acknowledged, almost beyond comparison, and the remainder of the island is not less so. In the aspect it derives from the sea on the one side, and the great sound on the other, it contains a long and varied panorama of the picturesque in scenery, for the tourist and artist, etc.

Long Island has a length of really about one hundred and forty miles, although the common notions, and most of the geographies put it at only one hundred and twenty. The total length, as first mentioned, is of course the distance from the now world-wide celebrated Fort Lafayette, at the Narrows, to the Light House on Turtle Hill, at the extremity of Montauk Point, looking out into the sea. Over this stretch of land, there are all varieties of soil and appearance, from the gradually sloping eminences of the great City of Brooklyn itself, with its noble public edifices, the long line of palaces in its streets, and the commoner dwellings too, representing so many millions and scores of millions of pecuniary value, with the immensely greater interests of three hundred thousand throbbing human lives, on to the wide flat plains of Queens and Suffolk counties, toward the centre of the island, where the cattle and sheep used to browse in common, a great privilege for the poor man; and thus and then through the "brushy plains," on eastward among pine and cedar and dwarf oak, to the richer regions of eastern Suffolk County.

The breadth of Long Island is from ten to twenty miles —running broader at its western extremity, and narrower at its eastern. It has also belonging to it a retinue of smaller islands, one of them, however (east of Peconic Bay), nearly the size of Staten Island. The following are the names of these adjacents of our little continent:

North Brother	Shelter Island
South Brother	Gardiner's Island
Riker's Island	Fisher Island
Plumb Island	Robin's Island
Great Gull Island	etc., etc.
Little " "	

Then there are the long stretching beaches and sand-islands on the south side, adjacent to the ocean.

Upon the whole, the area of our territory would make a

very respectable figure among the crowd of smaller princi-
palities, or even the little kingdoms of the continent of
Eurcpe; amounting to about 1550 square miles, or 960,-
000 acres, with a population that in two or three more lustrums will exceed half a million, and in the life time of
persons now living will (in the opinion of the writer hereof)
exceed the present population, of either one of about three-
fourths of the States of the Union, or of Canada. This seems
a daring statement, but it is fully born out by a sifting of
figures, and an estimate, not to say of probabilities, but what
amounts to certainties.

The reader will perceive, in view of the foregoing facts,
that it is not so very preposterous for our politicians, when
they get within control of half-fun and half-whiskey, to draw
out grave programmes of the "secession" of Long Island
from the good old mother State of New York, and setting
her up as a "sovereign," on her own hook. The *State of*
PAUMANOK! with our own beauteous Brooklyn for the capital; and a live governor of her own, and a whole swarm of
legislators and executive personages, and lobby gentlemen,
and contractors, etc., etc., etc., etc! To be sure, there is
something very grand in the picture of all this; only our taxes
hereabout being already up to the hideously outrageous rate
of *two per cent.,* we do not feel like piling on the agony any
higher. Nor is "secession" likely to be popular or profitable
in these quarters, these times, or any future times. So we
fear we shall have to dismiss the scheme of the independent
State of Long Island, or Paumanok, as something that
serves very well, it may be, to write a paragraph about, but
would not do to try the scheme in the furnace of practical
work,—and so let well enough alone.

Of course the *personal* and *financial* interests of Long
Island are overwhelmingly concentrated here in Brooklyn.
Four fifths of the inhabitants of the whole territory belong

in this western corner alone. Of wealth, the proportion is perhaps not as great. For the valuation of the "landed interest" of the island can foot up an immense figure, when an estimate is made by a competent person, including the value of the farmhouses, buildings, stock, products, etc. We should think the farming interest of the three counties of our island, Kings, Queens, and Suffolk, would represent, at the lowest figure, $100,000,000. There are some farms in this county that represent $2000 an acre, and plenty of them that represent $1000 an acre, and are good for the annual interest on that amount to their owners.

Then the fishing, eeling, clamming and fowling interests of the island, for over a hundred miles along the south bays, from Gravesend to Easthampton, stand for a large and solid value, affording a good living to hundreds and thousands of families, and an unfailing supply to the city markets.

The Great South Bay, as it is called, affords of itself a capital theme for one of these papers, which we shall take an early opportunity to furnish. How few of the million of inhabitants of New York and Brooklyn know anything about that inexhaustible sea-mine, full of treasures, that are really worth as much as the mines of California. There it stretches along, affording a safe and sheltered navigation for many a smack and sloop and village "packet." There, too, is Rockaway beach, so white and silvery, calm and pleasant, enough, perhaps, with its long-rolling waves in summer, sounding musically soft against the hard sand; yet how many a ship has met her death-wreck, driven on those sands, in the storms of winter.

We intend to devote this paper of our series to a statement of the origin of the Brooklyn Fire Department, which dates back to a period before the time of the Revolutionary War—was interrupted by that event—and then, immediately after peace, was resumed again, and has been prosperously carried on ever since. We shall give some valuable reminiscences, and an account of the earliest large fire in Brooklyn.

To those interested in our Fire Department (and who is not?) it will be curious to note the following, in which is recorded the first attempt, or nucleus, from which has been formed what is now one of the noblest and most effective departments in the United States.

It appears that the origin of the Fire Department of Brooklyn dates as far back as the year 1772, previous to the Revolutionary War. The following is one of the memoranda, for which we are indebted to the late Jeremiah Johnson:

At a town meeting held at Brookland on the 7th day of April, Anno Domini 1772, being the first Tuesday of said month, and then and there chose six firemen, according to audit of the Governor, Council, and General Assembly; an act for the more effectual extinguishment of fires near the ferry in the township of Brooklyn, in Kings County, passed the 31st December, 1768

The persons chosen for firemen are as follows:

Joseph Sharpe, John Crawley, Matthew Gleaves, Joseph Prior, John Middagh, Wm. Boerum.

We think the members of our Department, in their beautiful hall in Henry Street, ought to preserve some enduring memorial of these six original Brooklyn firemen. They commenced a work which is more to their credit, humble, as it is, than many a more talked-of class of persons.

111

The next year we hear of anything being done is after the war. For we suppose that during the Revolution men's minds were engaged in such momentous questions, and everything was so unsettled, that they gave little attention to safety from lesser dangers. In 1785, after the close of the war, there was a meeting of the villagers of Brooklyn, at the house of Mrs. Moser, at which an effective beginning was again made (probably the whole attempt had been suffered to go to decay during the war), for continuing the organization of a Fire Department. A Fire Company was formed, consisting of seven members, for one year; namely, Henry Stanton, captain; Abram Stoothoff, John Doughty, jr., Thomas Havens, J. Van Cott, and Martin Woodward.

The meeting just alluded to seems to have had official standing, as a regular meeting of freeholders; for they voted to raise a hundred and fifty pounds to purchase a fire engine —which vote was duly carried out.

This engine, if it were only now in existence, entire, would be almost as great a curiosity as anything in Barnum's Museum—especially to our fire laddies. It was manufactured in New York (up to this time fire engines had been imported from England), by Jacob Boome; and was one of the first, if not the first, made in the United States.

The above engine stood about three feet in height, was eight feet in length, three in width, and two and a half in depth. It was what is termed a long-stroke engine, and worked easy, throwing a stream 60 feet, through a pipe of three-quarter inch nozzle, of six feet length. Neither hose nor suctions were used, the supply of water being furnished in buckets, by hand, poured into the box. The box held 180 gallons. The arms were placed fore and aft. Eight men were sufficient to man this machine, which, like the venerable simile of the singed cat, was a good deal better than it looked.

With the above described engine, and the names as before given, commenced, or rather was resumed, the formal outset of the Brooklyn Fire Department, under the name of "Washington Company No. 1," which is the same identical No. 1 that has descended to the present day (Prospect Street), by being continued and passed along—few of the members of the present company, we dare say, having a correct idea of the antiquity and respectability of their beginning so far back as 1785. We have to add that the original house was located in Front Street, near Fulton. It is now in Prospect Street, near Main.

Nor must we forget to record that for many years there was dignity and prestige about the position of fireman that made a membership in the company carefully scanned, and duly weighed, before it was bestowed. Membership was an elective office. The firemen were chosen annually in town meeting; and the choice was considered something to be proud of.

At the town meeting in 1788, the number of firemen was increased to eleven, and the following were elected members: Stephen Baldwin, Captain; Benj. Baldwin, Silas Betts, Thomas Havens, Joseph Stevens, Gilbert Van Mater, John Doughty, jr., and John Van Cott. These members continued with little or no variation for the three succeeding years.

In 1794, it was resolved, in town meeting, to purchase a new engine, and a hundred and ninety pounds were voted for that purpose. With this, a much improved engine was procured, made in New York by Hardenbrook. The same year, the offices of clerk and treasurer of the Fire Department were instituted, and John Hicks unanimously chosen to perform the duties of both.

In 1795, the number of firemen was increased to thirty. By law each dwelling-house in Brooklyn was required to be provided with two fire-buckets, at the expense of the house-holders, and kept always ready for use, under a penalty.

Soon after this the villagers resolved to procure a fire-bell. Fifty pounds was raised for that purpose, and the bell, being bought and brought over to Brooklyn, was raised on top of a stone house belonging to Jacob Remsen, at the corner of what is now Fulton and Front streets (now Long Island Insurance Company's premises). Here, the bell being placed, Mr. Remsen agreed to see that it was duly rung on occasion of fires, and for his liberality, he was elected a member of the Fire Department, without being expected to do any other service.

We should like to trace out the present location of this bell; for we have a strong suspicion that it is yet in existence here in Brooklyn. When the old stone house was torn down (about the year 1818), the bell was removed to Middagh, near Henry Street; and then afterwards to the building called the "Eastern Market" in Sands Street, between Bridge and Gold—which building was afterwards converted into a church, and the bell used for that. Who is there that can give us any reliable information of this first old fire-bell used to alarm the villagers of Brooklyn?

All this while, by virtue of the statute passed by the Legislature in 1788, although a Brooklyn fireman received no pay, yet not only his position as we have intimated was considered a most honorable one, but he was exempted from "serving on the highways" (mending and repairing the roads), and from jury and inquest duty, and also from militia duty, except, as now, in case of invasion or other imminent danger.

In 1793, there were about seventy-five buildings within the fire-district of Brooklyn. These were, the majority of them, so near the Old Ferry, that water was relied upon to be obtained from the river.

We are unable to give minute details of the continuation of the growth of the Department in our town. We will transcribe, however, an account of one of the largest fires that occurred in Brooklyn in the earliest part of the present century—probably the largest and most destructive that ever occurred here up to its date, or during a number of years afterward. It occurred on the 16th of November, 1806. We are indebted to the only paper published in Brooklyn at the time, the *Long Island Intelligencer* (a weekly paper before described in this series) for a brief account of the cause of the fire, and the destruction caused by it. Then, just the same as now, incendiarism was rife. For the origin of the fire is given as follows:

The most uncommon hardihood and depravity was exhibited by two boys, named Wm. Cornwell and Martin Hill (neither of them exceeding the age of fifteen), who wilfully and deliberately caused the conflagration. The candle went out three times before they accomplished their diabolical intent, and was as often renewed. During the fire they robbed an adjoining store of a considerable sum of money; and intended, when the wind answered their purpose, to set fire to a large barn, the property of Mr. Abiel Titus. They are committed for trial at the April session.

The amount of loss incurred by this fire is not stated in money but it must have been considerable, according to the following list destroyed:

Two stables, a granary and several outhouses belonging to Mr. Suydam, who also lost a horse and a quantity of grain, salt and hay.

One large house (in which several families resided, who nearly lost their all) belonging to the estate of J. Van Nostrand, deceased.

One house belonging to Mr. Foster.

One house belonging to J. Garrison, Esq., torn down to prevent the extension of the flames.

One barn and out-house, the property of Mr. G. Hicks.

One stable belonging to B. Cornwell.
One barn belonging to Mrs. Carpenter.
One barn and soap works, the property of Mr. Burdett Stryker,
much damaged.

This excessive fire (for those days) caused of course a
good deal of excitement and dissatisfaction with the existing
condition of the fire apparatus.—For although the organization of the Department is alluded to as taking place more
than thirty years previously, the reader must not imagine
anything like the systematic provisions made now-a-days for
extinguishing fires. In those times they had only the two fire-
engines before mentioned. But the main reliance consisted
simply in buckets, passed along a string of people, from
hand to hand! Perhaps in addition, they had a few axes and
a couple of ladders. Of course, this will seem almost ridicu-
lous to our modern Brooklyn fire laddies, with their costly
and beautiful machines. But the just-mentioned fire aroused
the villagers of Brooklyn to procure another engine and
additional safeguards. The *Intelligencer* of a week or two
after has the following local paragraph of proceedings at a
meeting called:

Messrs. B. Birdsall, J. Doughty, J. Patchen, W. Clark and B.
Clark, were appointed a committee to inquire into the probable cost of
a large fire engine and bell, and such implements as they may conceive
to be useful for the purpose of extinguishing fires in the village of
Brooklyn, and to report thereon to a meeting of the inhabitants to be
called by them for that purpose.

This engine, according to all accounts, was duly procured,
and was the third fire-engine owned and possessed by the
good people of Brooklyn. We may as well add that we notice
in the proceedings at the meeting after the fire (as reported
in the *Intelligencer*) a resolution of thanks to the firemen of

New York, who came over and rendered valuable assistance in subduing the Brooklyn conflagration.

We may have more to say of the history of the Brooklyn Fire Department, bringing it down to the present day, in another number.

XV

THE APPRENTICES LIBRARY

ITS ORIGIN—CORNER STONE LAID IN 1825, BY LAFAYETTE

THE DAY AND THE SCENE—THE PUBLIC CEREMONIES—THE VETERANS

LAFAYETTE ASSISTING THE CHILDREN

UNEARTHING OF THE CORNER STONE, AND THE OLD DOCUMENTS

BROOKLYN OFFICIALS OF FORMER DAYS

PASTORS OF CHURCHES, ETC.

THE OLD CORNER STONE RELAID IN THE PRESENT ARMORY, AND THE DOCUMENTS DEPOSITED AGAIN

THE HANDS OF LAFAYETTE HAVE CONSECRATED THIS EDIFICE.

The premises at the corner of Henry and Cranberry streets, now the City Armory Building, resounding these times to the clash of arms, and the nightly orders of the drill-officers, are probably more rich with historical interest than the hundreds of young men who congregate there to learn soldiering have any idea of. This was the spot occupied, until 1858, by the three-story edifice known as the Apprentices Library. Clustering around the last-named establishment, and forming part of its authentic records, are so many points of importance in the past of Brooklyn that we have determined to make it the subject of one of our papers.

The Apprentices Library Building was for many years the Municipal Hall of Brooklyn. It was here the City Fathers met, and transacted the business of the public. Here, too, was the Post Office of Brooklyn. The County Clerk's apartments were in the same edifice, and in the upper story the judges of several courts from time to time held their sessions. The reason of its being called the Apprentices Library was that a few benevolent gentlemen, some forty years since, had combined together to establish a free library for youths and mechanics; and the enterprise led to their contributing money to put up the edifice which afterwards went by that name. It was intended (so we have been informed by old citizens) that the whole building, when completed, should gradually be devoted to purposes akin with that of the free library, such as educational improvement, lectures, studies appropriate for mechanics, etc. But this was never carried out, for some reason or another; probably because it was found that the building turned out to be a very handsome pecuniary investment, and returned to its owners, eventually, almost cent. per cent. from its increased value and central position.

The corner stone of the building was laid in 1825. The writer of these sketches, who was at that time a lad in his seventh year, remembers the occasion perfectly well, having been present at it. It was on the Fourth of July. The famous Lafayette was then on his last visit to America—the fourth, we believe. It was a historical event, that last visit, full of solemnity, as most of the old soldiers were dead. A few old veterans still remained, and gathered around Lafayette, here in Brooklyn and New York, at this last visit. Well do we, casting our mind back as we write, remember the scene, now more than thirty-five years ago—the group of bent, thin-faced, white-haired, old-fashioned fellows that were drawn together here in Brooklyn, on that occasion, and who met Lafayette when he came over the ferry. It was early in the forenoon. The weather was very fine. All the school and Sunday school children of Brooklyn were congregated at the lower end of Fulton Street, and marshalled into two lines, facing inward, with a wide space between them. Lafayette landed from the boat, in an old-fashioned yellow coach, and passed through these lines of little children (of which the present writer was one).

All the principal persons and officers of Brooklyn, of course, with Joshua Sands, the President of the Board of Trustees, had gathered at Fulton, then better known as Old Ferry—the Revolutionary veterans, if we remember right, being entertained in the meantime at Coe S. Downing's inn, then a well-known public-house on the east side of the street, between Front Street and the ferry.

Lafayette, with his hat off, rode slowly through the lines of children and the crowd that was gathered on the walks, and that looked at him and cheered him, from the houses, all the way up. After he had passed along ahead, to where Market Street now is, the carriage stopped, and the children, officers, citizens, etc., formed behind in procession, and followed him up to the corner of Henry and Cranberry streets, where the operation of laying the corner stone, was to be performed by Lafayette himself; he, having been invited, obligingly consented to execute the work. When arrived there, he alighted from his carriage, and, in the centre of a group of veterans and some of the functionaries of Brooklyn, he awaited the arrival, and getting in order, of the children and the rest of the procession. The excavation, etc., for the foundation walls and basement of the proposed building was quite rough, and there were heaps of stone and earth around, as was to be expected in such cases. Everything was more informal than it would be now, and as the children arrived, there was a little delay in getting them into safe and eligible places—whereupon many of the citizens volunteered to lift the smaller fry down the banks of the cellar, and place them on safe positions, etc., so that they might have a fair share in the view and hearing of the exercises. As most of the group around Lafayette were assisting in this work, the old companion of Washington, while waiting the signal to begin, pleasantly took it into his head to aid the same work himself, as he was in a place where there were a number of lads and lassies, waiting their turn to be lifted down. As good luck would have it, the writer of this series was one of those whom Lafayette took in his arms, and lifted down to be provided with a standing place; and proud enough as he was of it at the time, it may well be imagined with what feelings the venerable gentleman recollects it now.

There was quite an amount of speechifying, and, we suppose interchange of compliments of the usual nature; after which they took Lafayette riding out on the Heights and round the city. This was the last time Lafayette ever saw these shores—being, we believe, his fourth visit. Twice he came during the Revolutionary War, once a few years after the close of the war, and the establishment of independence.

Of course, we repeat, it is one of the dearest of the boyish memories of the writer that he not only saw, but was touched by the hands, and taken a moment to the breast of the immortal old Frenchman.

The corner stone then and there laid was a slab about thirty inches long, eighteen broad, and eight inches thick, enclosing and covering a small cavity or chest formed of brick, stone and mortar, in which were deposited various local memoranda and items that the child, in his seventh year, after seeing them thus deposited in '25, was singularly permitted to behold again when a man in his fortieth year: for in '58 the old Apprentices Library was taken down to make room for the present City Armory and the relics and current memoranda of the period of the first building, and of the visit of Lafayette, were unearthed again, and, after lying so long in darkness, once more, for a brief period, revisited the glimpses of the moon.

It will be well worth while to make a few minutes of these documents, which may perhaps one day become a precious record for antiquarians. There was a village Manual and Directory among the relics (printed at the office of Alden Spooner) from which we glean the names of the following officers, chosen at the just preceding election in May, 1825:

President of the Board of Trustees—Joshua Sands.

Trustees—John Doughty, John Moser, David Anderson, Joseph Sprague.

Assessors—William A. Sale, Jeremiah Mills, Benjamin Meeker.

Clerk to Board—John Dikeman.

State Commissioner—J. D. Conklin.

Health Physician—J. G. T. Hunt.

Weighers—G. P. Pease, John Titus, Andrew Tombs, R. W. Doughty.

Measurer—Henry Van Brunt.
Measurer of Lime—W. A. Sale.

The above officers were not elected, but appointed by the Board of Trustees.

We now come to the Fire Department of thirty-six years ago, in Brooklyn, as recorded in these relics:

Chief Engineer—John Doughty.
Vice President of Incorporated Firemen—Joshua Sutton.
Secretary—Richard Cornell.
Collector—Michael Trappel.

The names of a number of other officers at the time are also given, among which are the following, civil, military, naval, etc.:

Post Master of Brooklyn—Thomas Kirk.
Commander at the Navy Yard—Commodore Chauncey.
President L. I. Bank—Leffert Lefferts.
Cashier of the same—Daniel Embury.

The militia seems to have consisted of but one regiment, the 64th Infantry, of Kings County, with the following officers:

Colonel—Robert Nichols, of Brooklyn.
Lieutenant Colonel—John Lott, Jr., of Flatlands.
Major—William R. Dean, of Brooklyn.
Adjutant—James W. Smith, Brooklyn.
Quarter Master—Barnet Johnson, Wallabout.
Paymaster—Samuel Garrison, Gravesend.
Surgeon—Cornelius Dubois, New Utrecht.
Surgeon's Mate—Adrian Vanderveer, Flatbush.
Serjeant Major—William Jenkins.

Among those connected with the local institutions are the following head men:

President Brooklyn Fire Insurance Co.—William Furman.
Secretary—Freeman Hopkins.
President Medical Society—Joseph G. T. Hunt.
President Bible Society—Joshua Sands.
President Brooklyn Gas Light Co.—Fanning C. Tucker.

Among the church statistics we find the following:

Pastor Reformed Dutch Church—The Reverend Selah Woodhull.
Rector St. Ann's—The Reverend H. U. Onderdonk.
Sands St. Methodist—The Reverend Thomas Burch.
First Presbyterian—The Reverend Joseph Sandford. (This is the same church and premises, now occupied by The Reverend Henry Ward Beecher's Society.)
Jay St. Roman Catholic Church—Rev. John Farnham.
African Methodist Episcopal Church—Rev. William Quinn.

We dare say that in looking over these names, our few remaining elder citizens will have their memories carried back very easily to those times, and will without difficulty call up the personal appearance and manners of many of the above mentioned ministers and official functionaries. We can almost see some of them as we write. Old Josey Moser, for instance, dressed in drab clothes, goes along with his peculiar gait, round-shouldered, clean-shaved, or sits in his place in the Methodist church, from which he is never absent of a Sunday, rain or shine.

The old Apprentices Library being torn down to make

room for the present Armory (which we suppose will in its day in the future have to fall to make room for something else), the stone which capped and held safe the above relics was carefully preserved, and in 1858, when the Armory foundation was laid, it was duly put in its new corner, and now forms a part of the existing building. It is a valuable memento, and our citizens should be more generally aware of its history, as identified with the foregoing narrative. That stone has been touched by the almost sacred hands of Lafayette, and is therefore hallowed by associations that, as time rolls on, will every year become more and more precious.

Of the above mentioned records and memoranda in the old cavity, and in a glass bottle inclosed in it, we believe they were all of them in sufficient preservation to be added to the deposits in the cavity under the corner stone of the present Armory building.

One of the most useful and humane of all the institutions of our city, namely the hospital in Raymond Street, receives within its benevolent walls about thirteen hundred persons in the course of a year, and though it preserves the character, in the main, of a pay hospital, it has also the character, in proper cases, of a free institution, as far as possible. We understand that the embarrassments in the way of making it entirely free are such that the existing plan has been found necessary, for many important reasons.

The first attempt at a regular public hospital, within the limits of Brooklyn, was about the year 1844. Many of our readers will remember the building at that time used for the purpose. It was a large old mansion, appropriately of a light yellow color, in Hudson Avenue (then Jackson Street), and had been the residence of Clarence D. Sackett, Esq. It was situated on elevated ground, a little back from the street, and was surrounded by a roomy garden. This was used for two or three years (1844, '5 etc.).

It is to be mentioned, however, that on the breaking out of cholera, or any violent epidemic, at intervals, for a great many years previous, temporary hospitals were always provided. The last of this kind was during the cholera season of some thirteen years ago, and was in a large frame building adjacent to the northwest corner of Lafayette and Raymond streets.

But it was soon found that the ordinary house accommodations in Hudson Avenue were going to be altogether insufficient for what was required; and an attempt was made to do something worthy of the city. Gatherings were called in the churches, and subscriptions sought in every direction. But Brooklyn had not the wealth and public spirit it has now; and the subscriptions were very slack. To urge on matters Augustus Graham, continuing the princely liberality that has made his name venerated in so many directions among us, engaged to give for a new hospital the sum of $30,000, on condition that a like sum should be raised among other parties. In the meantime a charter of incorporation had been obtained (1845) from the Legislature.

As there appeared, after trial, very little prospect of obtaining from the public the outside $30,000, as required by Mr. Graham, the directors and a few warm friends of the project put their hands in their own pockets and raised a great part of the needed sum. Mr. Graham also revoked the conditions. Upon that the work was considered secure.

Grounds being purchased (those at present occupied), west of Washington Park, and a plan having been settled on, the corner stone of the Brooklyn City Hospital was laid in the summer of 1851, and the edifice sufficiently advanced for occupancy and use in the following April, when it was formally opened. Only one wing was completed; the other was left to be built when wanted.

Since then the remaining wing has been added (in 1855), and many other improvements made. The building now presents, from its elevated and beautiful site, a noble appearance, on Raymond Street, a little north of De Kalb Avenue.

Those who have had to do with the establishment of this hospital may well be satisfied with its present (1862) state of completeness. The entire structure consists of a main or central building, with extensions on the north and south side and presents a front of two hundred feet in length, by fifty-five feet in depth, and is capable of accommodating three hundred patients. The position of the hospital is one of the finest, and best adapted to the purpose for which it was erected, that could probably be selected. The court-yard is of ample dimensions, and is laid out in walks and ornamented with trees and shrubbery, while the whole is surrounded with an iron railing. In the rear is Washington Park.

The first floor of the main building contains the trustees'

room, office, dining-room and store room, the latter provided with every requisite, and everything arranged and
kept in a neat and systematic manner. The second floor contains two rooms for the superintendent's family, one room for
the house surgeon, one ward dispensary, etc. On the third
floor are three private rooms for lady and gentleman patients, with another apartment for the house physician. The
fourth floor contains two wards. In the rear of the central
building is the kitchen, divided from the other portion of the
house by a wide entry. It contains two ranges, and is neat
and tidy in appearance, notwithstanding the cooking for the
whole establishment is done here.

The north wing is divided off into wards, both medical
and surgical. The extreme northern part is allotted to col-
ored persons.

The south wing is four stories in height. The first floor is
divided off into four wards each, about 35 feet square, with
a ceiling 14 feet in the clear. These are intended for private
patients. At the extreme end is a large corridor, provided
with bath rooms, etc. A hall 9 feet wide divides the wards
from an apartment in the rear, which is fitted up for a laun-
dry and is heated by two large furnaces. The other floors are
similarly divided, and the whole is capable of accommodating about 200 patients.

The entire building is heated by means of hot-air furnaces, is well ventilated, and every apartment is kept scrupu-
lously neat and clean.

The whole of the establishment remains under charge of
Dr. Nichols, well known for some years past as the superintendent. We take this opportunity of acknowledging the
genuine courtesy of Dr. Nichols toward us, and cheerfully
showing us around the wards, etc., during our visits in time
past.

It may be as well to mention, in this place, that no case of small-pox, or other infectious diseases, are received at this hospital—there being special provision made for them by the county authorities, at Flatbush.

As our readers will no doubt be pleased to hear the exact statistics of the Brooklyn City Hospital, we subjoin them for the year lately closed, 1861:

Whole number who have received the benefits of the hospital for the year		1256
Of whom were cured	672	
Relieved	220	
Discharged at their own request	50	
Disorderly or eloped	120	
Died	70	
Remaining 1st of January, 1862	124	
The number who paid in whole or in part is	1038	
Wholly charity	218	
		1256

Of the 70 deaths, 37 were Coroner's cases from accidents, leaving the actual number from disease, etc. 33.

Out of those who paid on entering, 26 became charity and remained such on an average 57 days each.

Of the charity patients, 173 were accidents sent by the city. The average time of each accident was 57 days, making for those sent by the city to a total of 1409 weeks, which at $3 per week is $4,227.

The whole number of rations issued during the year is 59,591.

XVII

OUR CITY TWENTY-FIVE YEARS AHEAD

THE SAME, TWENTY-FIVE YEARS AGO

FULTON STREET NEAR THE OLD FERRY

SANDS STREET METHODIST CHURCH

WELL KNOWN STORES, ETC.

THE OLD LOG CABIN

WELL KNOWN OLD SETTLERS AND
FAMILIES—A RUNNING LIST OF
THEIR NAMES

A REFLECTION

The child is already born, and is now living, stout and hearty, who will see Brooklyn numbering one million inhabitants! Its situation for grandeur, beauty and salubrity is unsurpassed probably on the whole surface of the globe; and its destiny is to be among the most famed and choice of the half dozen of the leading cities of the world. And all this, doubtless, before the close of the present century.

And while we thus give a prospective glance twenty-five or thirty years ahead, to a period which will "take care of itself," we will occupy this paper of our series with a retrospective glance at certain matters, little or large (as the reader may choose to consider them), which involve the condition of Brooklyn twenty-five and thirty years ago. Our city grows so fast that there is some danger of the events and incidents of more than ten years gone being totally forgotten. Twenty-five or thirty years ago, who would have expected such a mighty increase as has already come upon us—with the prospect, nay, the certainty of the million population just alluded to?

Around the ferries, thirty years ago, the scene presented was of course a very different one, from now. There were only three, the Old Ferry (the present Fulton), the New Ferry (at the foot of Main Street), and the remaining one at the foot of Jackson Street (now Hudson Avenue).

Fulton Street below Henry Street was considerably narrower than it is now. It was widened to its present size somewhere about the year 1835. Previous to that period, it presented much the appearance of a bustling country town— and partially "alive," most of the time, with market and fish wagons, and their proprietors, come in from miles up the island, with their produce, intended for the New York or Brooklyn markets. But we must reserve a more particular description of this lower and important portion of our city, at that time clustering around the Old Ferry, for another article of our series.

Ascending to Sands Street, the upper corner on Fulton was occupied for ever so many years by a venerable and stately drug-store, the principal one in the village. Where the present roomy and handsome, though plain, brick church for the Methodists stands, was then a wooden church,—the most crowded place of worship in the place, and the scene of Rev. John N. Maffit's greatest triumphs and excitements. The Washington Street church was not built then. The wooden church in Sands Street was, as we have said, very crowded, every Sunday—and indeed almost every night during the week. That was the time of "Revivals." A third of the young men in Brooklyn, particularly the mechanics and apprentices, and young women of the same class in life (and O, what pretty girls some of them were!) "experienced religion," as it is still called. In many cases it was no doubt a reality; but in many, alas! it was an ebullition of the moment; and as such soon became "backsliders." The hearty old Methodist tunes that are now sung so generally had then "just come out," and they were given with enormous fervor. The galleries of the church were often sprinkled with the mischievous ones who came to ridicule and make sport; but even here the arrows of prayer and pleading sometimes took effect. Many who came to scoff were irresistibly drawn up to the altar, and spent the night in tears and mental wrestling. How many of our readers will recollect that old wooden church? How many will remember being present in it, and witnessing the scenes above described?

Just on the turn of the west side of Fulton Street, thirty years since, was the most frequented drug-store in Brooklyn, kept by Mr. Vanderhoef. Dr. Ball (father of the late Police Physician), had his office there; and Dr. Wendell, too, we believe. Those two were the court physicians then; more omnipotent than eastern pachas. Can any body who reads this call to mind of having a tooth drawn, or any surgical operation performed, in Vanderhoef's back room? It makes the writer shudder, even now, to think of the diabolical array of cold steel that room presented! Over the way was one of the few dry goods stores in the place, kept by Mr. C. E. Bill.

On the lower corner of Cranberry Street and Fulton was Terence Riley's grocery—a famous resort for the buyers of butter and sugar by the pound, and potatoes by the small measure. On the opposite side above, third door below Nassau Street, stood one of the oldest buildings in the country. The tradition was that it had been occupied by General Putnam, before the Battle of Long Island. (But then every old house has some tradition.) Samuel E. Clements occupied it as the post office, and as the printing establishment of the *Long Island Patriot,* the Democratic organ. On the second floor, old Mr. Hartshorne had a little stationery store, and a case where he set up types for the *Patriot.* Mr. Hartshorne died in December, 1859, at a very advanced age. He was every way a remarkable man, and a credit to the craft. We have spoken of him in a previous number of this series.

On the upper corner of Orange and Fulton was a comfortable but old fashioned wooden dwelling, occupied by a well-known Brooklynite, Losee Van Nostrand. From that, up to where the Presbyterian church at the commencement of Clinton Street now is, the grounds were open, and shaded in front by magnificent elm trees. James B. Clarke had an ample house and grounds where Pineapple now cuts in. On the opposite side, between Oakes and Parson's cabinet store and the corner of Concord Street, was a large wooden building, erected for a theatre and circus. Plays and equestrian performances of a second-rate character were given there at intervals for about a year, but then discontinued. The building was then altered into dwellings—and subsequently into stores also. All were swept away by the great fire of '48.

But we must not forget the old one-story house on the east upper corner of Nassau Street, with the tough mulberry trees in front. That was a quaint old house indeed. What boy of those days but remembers the pleasant-faced and lady-like females, and the air of domestic comfort and hospitality that marked that old house? Then the mulberrys, which the good natured occupants allowed all the idle children to get; and in the getting, how many brickbats and stones fell in dangerous proximity to passengers' heads.

On the upper corner of Cranberry and Fulton, was an ancient edifice occupied as a grocery store by Mr. Conover, and Mr. Barkaloo. That was where Hall's buildings stood before the fire of '48. Mrs. Hayes, over the way, kept a confectionery shop, first at the second door below Nassau Street. She died not long since, at an advanced age.

The old log cabin, famous in the days of '40, was the fourth door above Orange Street, on the west side of Fulton.

Thirty years! what changes have indeed come over Brooklyn in that time! How comparatively few who were then active and ambitious here, still remain among us. Many have died and many have moved away. The population of Brooklyn was then but eighteen or twenty thousand. Now it is more than twelve times that number.

Then the old and well-known citizens of Brooklyn—let us see if we can't call up the names of some of those old "stand by's"—though we dare say we shall forget many. Not many are now living. Hardly a place in the United States, not even the oldest and most "moral" settlements of New England, can boast a better list of these citizens of integrity and general worth. We have mentioned the names of many of these, in a former paper of our series, but it will do no harm to go over it again, and increase the list. We have to specify Gen. Johnson, Rev. E. M. Johnson, Joseph Sprague, Alden Spooner, Judge Murphy, Henry Waring, Losee Van Nostrand, Dr. Wendell, Messrs. Adrian Hegeman, Gabriel Furman, Joseph Moser, and Mr. Browne, Mr. S. Carman (the watch-maker), Mr. Pelletrau, Edward (Mayor) Copeland, Messrs. John Dikeman, William M. Udall, Conklin Brush (Mayor), James Walters, Samuel Smith (Mayor), Mr. Eastabrook, Joshua Rogers, R. V. W. Thorne, Samuel Fleet, ex-Mayors Smith and Hall (not then ex-Mayors, however), D. Coope, Colonel Manning, Gen. Underhill, and J. W. Lawrence. Then there were the Garrisons, Bergens, Doughtys, Barbarins, Sandses, Sacketts, Polhemuses, Rushmores, Engles, Cornells, Merceins, Stantons, Suydams, Baches, Tredwells, Carters, Hickses, Schencks, Schoonmakers, Smiths, Storys, Degraws, Willoughbys, Princes, Romaines, Grahams, Packers, Bartows, Howlands, Lows, Arculariuses, Van Brunts, Lotts, Martenses, Wyckoffs, Conselyeas, Vanderbilts, Jacksons, Debevoises, Coleses, Thornes, Nichollses, Cortelyous, and so forth. Children or descendants of these are still flourishing among us. Mr. Thomas Kirk, Fanning C. Tucker, Jonathan Trotter (Mayor), Ralph Malbone, Samuel Boughton, D. Anderson, and Mr. Birch (the former editor), are additional names recalled to us in the hurry of writing.

Who remembers old Mr. Langdon and his wheeled chair, which he used to sit on in front of the Franklin house (at the ferry) guarding his gouty foot from harm? Who of our readers will recollect "the last of the Leather-breeches," old Mr. Patchen? or those other respectable citizens, Zachariah Lewis, Abraham Vanderveer, Mr. Moon, the lumber dealer, Mr. Hadden, Coe S. Downing, James B. Clarke, Tunis Joralemon, H. E. Pierrepont, Mr. Phillips (the baker), old Mr. Worthington (the Postmaster), Dr. Hunt, and Leffert Lefferts?

We have thus run over, at random, some of the reminiscences of persons, localities and events in the Brooklyn of twenty-five or thirty years ago.

Ah, if these occurrences, and the foregoing names are perused by any of the remaining old folks, their contemporaries, we (then a boy of twelve years) have jotted down, above, they will surely have some curious, perhaps melancholy reflections.

XVIII

THE NEW COURT HOUSE

REMINISCENCES OF THE NEIGHBORHOOD

THE FARMS AND ORCHARDS, ETC.

LAND SPECULATIONS

PARMENTIER'S GARDEN

THE HESSIAN HOSPITAL

MILITARY AND OTHER PUBLIC GARDENS
OF OLD TIMES

A POLITICAL MEETING OF FORTY
YEARS AGO

LOCAL MAGNATES FORMERLY

We will devote this paper of our series to some incidents connected with the locality of our new County Court House and Supervisors' Building, opposite the City Hall, on the site occupied and known during the earlier sixty years of this century as the Military Gardens.

We ought to premise that the region surrounding our City Hall, and this new building being put up for the courts of the county, supervisors, etc., is not only of deep interest to the inhabitants of Brooklyn, from its political connexions, but from hundreds of old local historical associations.

The line of Fulton Street up to this point, and so on to the junction of Fulton and Flatbush avenues is the original road, pretty much the same now as it has been from the settlement of Brooklyn over two hundred years ago.

The neighborhood of our City Hall was, even in old times, a sort of central spot, where the people of Brooklyn, and the county, met to transact business, or, on the Sabbath, for religious worship.

The original old Brooklyn church, under the Dutch settlement, was in this section, on Fulton Avenue, right in the middle of the road, near where Duffield Street now comes out. Here, for two or three ages, the settlers of Brooklyn and of Flatlands, Flatbush, and New Utrecht, as well as from the Old Ferry, and from the Wallabout, came on Sunday, to listen to sermons in Dutch. It is the same society, passed on by regular succession, that now worships in the church in Joralemon Street, adjoining Court.

There are plenty of people now living in Brooklyn who remember all this part of the city, as it was laid out in farms, orchards, gardens, etc. It used to help to supply the New York market with garden vegetables, just as Flatbush and the other outer towns do now.

Here too, and branching off from here, have been the localities of some of the biggest land speculations ever known in our city. Just above here, at the spot long known as Parmentier's Garden, during the great speculation times of 1833, some shrewd fellows gave $57,000 for a small tract of ground, and immediately cut it up into "lots," and sold it off for nearly $100,000. It is probable it would not bring much more than that sum at this day. Brooklyn, however, has been full of similar speculations.

Among other points of interest in the neighborhood we are speaking of was an ancient two-story house, painted yellow in modern times, that stood on the west side of Fulton Street, nearly opposite the point now occupied by the Central Bank. This old house was of a date coeval with the Revolutionary War, and was principally noted as having been occupied, during many years of the war, by the British troops as a hospital. It went by the name of the "Hessian Hospital," within the recollection of the writer. It was on the site now occupied by the handsome stores just below the Mechanics Bank.

But we promised to say something about the premises now being substantially built upon for the new Court House. The original Military Garden was not the large edifice as our citizens have seen it, but the smaller building on the part of the premises to the west. This, we believe, was the identical framework of the edifice occupied there early in the present century, by an eccentric old landlord called Col. Greene, who had fought in the Revolution.

But old Col. Greene passed away, and other landlords, one after another, succeeded him. The large edifice, the eastern part of the Military Garden, was put up about 1826 or '7, by Mr. Duflon, a Swiss, who had come to Brooklyn and hired the premises on a long lease for a public house. The upper part of the new edifice, which was convenient and roomy, was used as a Masonic Lodge, for Masonry in those days occupied the same place in the public favor that Odd

Fellowship and kindred institutions have since. The premises still continued to be used for political purposes and for balls, public dinners, and had quite an handsome garden attached, with little summer houses.

These gardens, let us here remark, were a conspicuous feature in Brooklyn during the earlier part of the present century. Besides the one we are mentioning, there were some four or five others, all well known and well patronised, many of the visitors coming from New York, especially on holidays and Sundays. There was Brower's Garden, between what are now Pierrepont and Montague streets; part of its handsome trees and shrubbery remained until the spring of a year ago, but it is now all obliterated and covered with stores. However, Brooklyn had such a rural character that it was almost one huge farm and garden in comparison with its present appearance.

Off the west of the places we have alluded to, and adjacent to them, stretched the valuable properties in which, though unthought of at the time, lay treasures of speculation (as they have proved since) richer than a California gold mine. We allude to the Pierrepont estate and to the Joralemon and Remsen farms. Those stretched away down to the river, from the upper part of Fulton Street. In those days sales out of this property were made by the acre, and forty years ago, goodly portions of this valuable region might have been purchased at the rate of fifty dollars an acre! When we contrast this with the present price of from three to ten thousand dollars a city lot, it gives one some idea of Brooklyn progress.

The same premises in the neighborhood of our City Hall, and indeed the very ones where the Court House is going up, were used, in old times, for the political conventions, and town meetings of the people of Brooklyn, and for the general meetings of the county.

We will, in imagination, resume one of these old county meetings of 40 years ago. On the very ground of this Court House there would be a general gathering of villagers. One man, for instance, would be present whom everybody seemed to know, and to be friendly with. He was a man of good medium stature and size, with an unmistakable Dutch physiognomy, rather sharp nose, florid complexion, and robust form, dressed like a well-to-do farmer, and with an air of benevolence and good sense in all he said or did. That was Gen. Jeremiah Johnson, a legitimate representative and type of the true and original Hollandic stock that laid the foundation of Brooklyn and Kings County. Then among the crowd you would see the tall stout shoulders of Joseph Sprague, with his white head; and such citizens as Losee Van Nostrand, Abraham Vanderveer, and old Alden Spooner.

Here too from the earliest times, were "the polls" for election. Somewhat different were they from the elections of our day, in many respects, especially in the number of votes given. Fifty years ago the whole of Kings County gave less than 700 votes. Still there was the same eagerness, the same party rivalry—indeed we have heard old men say that the strife was far bitterer then than in these days. When a national or state election was held, however, it was a long time, sometimes several weeks, before the result was known with certainty.

So our readers will perceive that the future political associations of our new Court House, for all its newness, will be invested with an atmosphere of as much antiquity and of the personnel of primitive old Dutch Brooklyn character— (which gives a good smack to the breed) as the limited chronology of the American continent affords.

XIX

DOMESTIC LIFE OF THE EARLY
SETTLERS OF BROOKLYN

SCARCITY OF TIME-PIECES

THE HOUSES AND THEIR INTERIOR
ARRANGEMENTS

TEA PARTIES AND WOMEN'S VISITS

DRESS AND ORNAMENT

SPINNING WHEELS

WEALTH AND INTELLIGENCE OF THE
BROOKLYN DUTCH

The Dutch foundations of Brooklyn and of the towns of Kings County were laid so strongly and deeply by the first immigrants from Holland, and by the course of events during the period from 1620 to the close of the century, that they will without doubt continue to have a profound influence on the character of our region for ages and ages to come.

It will probably be better understood a long while hence that these Dutch foundations have been of equal importance with the English constituents of our national stock; although the latter, so far, are much the most talked of.

Long Island, though settled at this western end by the Dutch aforesaid, was always an object of envy to the English. In 1635, the latter, under the protection of Lord Stirling, attempted to make a settlement a ways down on the island, but Governor Kieft sent a force from New Amsterdam and drove them away.

Upon the English finally taking possession, there was no great change in the political status of the country here, beyond the formal wielding of power in the name of the British Monarch, instead of that of the Dutch Stadtholder. And as to any social or domestic change, it was positively unknown. And it is with reference to the latter, the social life of the colony, that we now make a few remarks.

The reader must not suppose, either, that the domestic life of the Colony of New Amsterdam was concentrated mainly on Manhattan Island, as it is at present. On the contrary, there were for many years considerably more actual inhabitants here in Brooklyn, Wallabout, Flatbush, New Utrecht and Bushwick than in all the rest of the colony of New York Island on the main land put together. So that a sketch of the peculiarities of the early domestic life of the Dutch settlers applies emphatically to this region of ours hereabout.

Nor is it so very long ago since the domestic habits of the people and families have changed to what is now the fashion. Up to a comparatively late date, you could here and there meet with old families that, in many respects, preserved the usages, furniture, simplicity, etc., of former times.

At the very first, the houses were mostly one story huts of logs.

But as the forests became cleared away, and the colony increased, the style of living experienced a material change, and the settlers commenced to build their houses of brick and stone. For some time [we are indebted for this and the following paragraphs to Mary L. Booth's excellent *History of the City of New York,*] the bricks were imported from Holland; in the administration of Stuyvesant, however, some enterprising citizens established a brick-yard on New York Island; and the material became henceforth popular in the colony. The northern part of the island furnished abundance of stone. Many of the wooden house and checker-work fronts, or rather gable ends of small black and yellow Dutch bricks, with the date of their erection inserted in iron figures, facing the street. Most of the houses, indeed, fronted the same way; the roofs were tiled or shingled, and invariably surmounted with a weathercock. The windows were small and the doors large; the latter were divided horizontally, so that, the upper half being swung open, the burgher could lean on the lower and smoke his pipe in peaceful contemplation. Not less comfortable were the social "stoeps," and the low projecting eaves, beneath which the friendly neighbors congregated at twilight to smoke their long pipes and discuss the price of beaver-skins. These institutions have come down to our own times, and are still known and appreciated in the suburbs of the city.

Every house was surrounded by a garden, varying in size according to the locality, but usually large enough to furnish accommodations for a horse, a cow, a couple of pigs, a score of barn-door fowls, a patch of cabbages, and a bed of tulips. . . .

Carpets, too, were almost unknown in the city up to the period of the Revolution. Now and then a piece of drugget ostentatiously dignified by the name of carpet, and made to serve for the purpose of a crumb-cloth, was found in the houses of the wealthiest burghers, but even these were not in general use. The snow-white floor was sprinkled with fine sand, which was curiously stroked with a broom into fantastic curves and angles. This adornment pertained especially to the parlor; a room that was only used upon state occasions. The first carpet said to have been introduced into the city was found in the house of the pirate, Kidd, this was merely a good-sized Turkey rug, worth about twenty-five dollars.

The most ornamental piece of furniture was usually the bed, with its heavy curtains and valance of camlet and killeminster. Mattresses were as yet unheard of; in their stead was used a substantial bed of live geese feathers, with a lighter one of down for a covering. These beds were the pride of the notable Dutch matrons; in these and the well-filled chests of homemade linen lay their claims to skill in housewifery.

The beds and pillows were encased in check coverings; the sheets were of home-spun linen, and over the whole was thrown a patchwork bed-quilt, made of bits of calico cut in every conceivable shape, and tortured into the most grotesque patterns that could possibly be invented by human ingenuity.

In a corner of the room stood a huge oaken, iron-bound chest, filled to overflowing with household linen, spun by the feminine part of the family, which they always delighted in displaying before visitors. At a later date, this gave place to the "chest of drawers" of our grandmothers' times—huge piles of drawers, placed one upon the other, and reaching to the ceiling, with brass rings over the key-holes to serve as knobs. The escritoire, too, with its complication of writing desk, drawers and mysterious pigeon-holes, came into use about the same time; but both of these were unknown to the genuine Knickerbockers.

. . . . Glass-ware was almost unknown; punch was drank in turns by the company, from a huge bowl, and beer from a tankard of silver. Sideboards were not introduced until after the Revolution, and were exclusively of English origin.

Sofas, couches, lounges, and that peculiarly American institution, the rocking-chair, were things unknown to our Dutch ancestors.

Their best chairs were of Russia leather, profusely ornamented with double and triple rows of brass nails, and so straight and high-backed as to preclude the possibility of a moment's repose. Besides these, the parlor was commonly decorated with one or two chairs with embroidered backs and seats, the work of the daughters of the family. . . . Mahogany had not yet come into use; nearly all the furniture was made of oak, maple or nutwood. . . .

Some half-dozen clocks were to be found in the settlement, with about the same number of silver watches; but as these were scarcely ever known to go, their existence was of very little practical consequence. No watchmaker had yet found it to his interest to emigrate, and the science of horology was at a low ebb in the colony. The flight of time long continued to be marked by sun-dials and hour-glasses; indeed, it is only since the Revolution that clocks have come into general use. . . .

. . . . Pictures were plentiful, if we may believe the catalogues of household furniture of the olden times; but these pictures were wretched engravings of Dutch cities and naval engagements, with family portraits at five shillings a head, which were hung at regular intervals upon the parlor walls. The window curtains were generally of flowered chintz, of inferior quality, simply run upon a string. . . .

Stoves were never dreamed of by the worthy Knickerbockers, but in their stead they had the cheerful fireplace—sometimes in the corner, sometimes extending almost across the length of the room—with its huge back-log, and glowing fire of hickory wood. The shovel and tongs stood, one in each corner, keeping guard over the brass-mounted andirons which supported the blazing pile. In front was the brass fender, with its elaborate ornaments; and a curiously wrought fire-screen stood in the corner. Marble mantels had never yet been thought of; but the chimney-pieces were inlaid with parti-colored Dutch tiles, representing all sorts of scriptural and apocryphal stories. The kitchen fire-places were less pretentious, and of an immense size, so large that they would almost have sufficed to roast an ox whole. Over the fire swung the hooks and trammels, designed for the reception of the immense iron cooking pots, long since superseded by the modern stoves and ranges. The children and negroes grouped in the spacious chimney corners, cracking nuts and telling stories by the light of the blazing pine knots, while the "vrouws" turned the spinning-wheel, and the burghers smoked their long pipes and silently watched the wreaths of smoke as they curled above their heads. At nine they regularly said their prayers, commended themselves to the protection of the good Saint Nicholas, and went to bed to rise with the dawn.

So regular was their lives that the lack of time-pieces made but little difference. The model citizens rose at cock-crowing, breakfasted with the dawn, and went about their usual avocations. When the sun reached the "noon-mark," dinner was on the table. This was strictly a family meal; dinner parties were unheard of, and the neighbor who should have dropped in without ceremony would have been likely to have met an indifferent welcome. But this apparent want of sociality was amply atoned for by the numerous tea-parties. After dinner the worthy Dutch matrons would array themselves in their best linsey-jackets and petticoats of their own spinning, and, putting a half-finished worsted stocking into the capacious pocket which hung down from their girdle, with their scissors, pin-cushion and keys outside their dress, sally forth to a neighbor's house to "take tea." Here they plied their knitting needles and their tongues at the same time, discussed the village gossip, settled their neighbors' affairs to their own satisfaction, and finished their stockings in time for tea, which was on the table at six o'clock precisely. This was the occasion for the display of the family plate and the Lilliputian cups of rare old china. out of which the guests sipped the fragrant bohea, sweetening it by an occasional bite from the huge lump of loaf sugar which was laid invariably by the side of each plate, while they discussed the hostess' apple-pies, doughnuts, and waffles. Tea over, the party donned their cloaks and hoods, for bonnets were not, and set out straightway for home in order to be in time to superintend the milking and look after their household affairs before bedtime.

As we have already said, the Dutch ladies wore no bonnets, but brushed their hair back from their foreheads and covered it with a close-fitting cap of muslin or calico; over this they wore, in the open air, hoods of silk or taffeta, elaborately quilted. Their dress consisted of a jacket of cloth or silk, and a number of short petticoats of every conceivable hue and material, quilted in fanciful figures. If the pride of the Dutch matrons lay in their beds and linen, the pride of the Dutch maidens lay equally in their elaborately wrought petticoats, which were their own handiwork, and usually constituted their only dowry. The wardrobe of a fashionable lady usually contained from ten to twenty of these, of silk, camlet, cloth, drugget, India stuff and a variety of other materials, all closely quilted, and costing from five to thirty dollars each. They wore blue, red, and green worsted stockings of their own knitting, with parti-colored clocks, together with high-heeled leather shoes. No finer material was known until after the Revolution. Considerable jewelry was in use among them in the shape of rings and brooches. Gold neck and fob chains were unknown: the few who owned watches attached them to chains of silver or steel; though girdle-chains of gold and silver were much in vogue among the most fashionable belles. These were attached to the richly bound Bibles and hymn-books and suspended from the belt outside the dress, thus forming an ostentatious Sunday decoration. For necklaces, they wore numerous strings of gold beads; the poorer classes, in humble imitation, encircled their throats with steel and glass beads, and strings of Job's tears, fruit of a plant which was famed to possess some medicinal virtues. . . .

. . . . Every household had from two to six spinning-wheels for wool and flax, whereon the women of the family expended every leisure moment. Looms, too, were in common use, and piles of home-spun cloth and snow-white linen attested to the industry of the active Dutch maidens. Hoards of home-made stuffs were thus accumulated in the settlement, sufficient to last till a distant generation.

Such were some of the peculiarities of domestic life in the Dutch settlement here on both sides of the river during the latter years of the 17th, and the whole of the 18th century.

The houses of the inhabitants of Brooklyn, Wallabout, Bedford, Gowanus, etc., and all through the line of what is now Fulton Street and Avenue, gradually assumed better and better proportions, and about a hundred years ago were of a character which would have been creditable to an old European rural town of the first class. There was a good deal of wealth and intelligence here, and the necessities of their occupations did not prevent them from devoting a part of their time to mental, social and religious matters.

If there be any who, in looking back to the periods and persons we are sketching, feel a sort of compassion for their supposed inferior chances and lower development, we advise them to spare their benevolence, and apply it where it would be more truly needed. For the comparison of merit between the inhabitants here during the last century, or of the years previous, with the present time, and all its vaunted educational and fashionable advantages, is not a whit in favor of our own day in all the important respects that make manly and womanly excellence.

XX

THE OLD RAILROAD TUNNEL AT
SOUTH FERRY

PICTURE OF THE TRAIN STARTING
IN FORMER DAYS

EAST NEW YORK AND BEDFORD

JAMAICA AND ITS IMPORTANCE

THE BRANCH AND HEMPSTEAD

THE GREAT PLAINS OF LONG ISLAND

HICKSVILLE AND SURROUNDINGS

FARMINGDALE AND ''THE BRUSH''

THE VALUABLE TRACTS THROUGH THIS
REGION OF THE ISLAND

We alluded in the last paper to the fact that though the inhabitants and wealth of Long Island were mostly concentrated in Brooklyn, there were still other sections, forming the vast remainder of the island, that were well worthy of record and of further investigation than has yet been afforded them by our local newspapers, or by any of the literary class hereabouts.

The old tunnel, that used to lie there under ground, a passage of Acheron-like solemnity and darkness, now all closed and filled up, and soon to be utterly forgotten, with all its reminiscences; of which, however, there will, for a few years yet be many dear ones, to not a few Brooklynites, New Yorkers, and promiscuous crowds besides. For it was here you started to go down the island, in summer. For years, it was confidently counted on that this spot, and the railroad of which it was the terminus, were going to prove the permanent seat of the business and wealth that belong to such enterprises. But its glory, after enduring in great splendor for a season, has now vanished—at least its old Long Island Railroad glory has. We were along there a few days since, and could not help stopping, and giving the reins for a few moments to an imagination of the period when the daily eastern train, with a long string of cars, filled with summer passengers, was about starting for Greenport, after touching at all the intermediate villages and depots. We are (our fancy will have it so), in that train of cars, ready to start. The bell rings, and winds off with that sort of a twirl or gulp (if you can imagine a bell gulping), which expresses the last call, and no more afterwards; then off we go. Every person attached to the road jumps on from the ground or some of the various platforms, after the train starts—which (so imitative an animal is man) sets a fine example for greenhorns or careless people at some future time to fix themselves off with broken legs or perhaps mangled bodies. The orange women, the newsboys, and the limping young man with long-lived cakes, look in at the windows with an expression that says very plainly, "We'll run alongside, and risk all the danger, while you find the change." The smoke with a greasy smell comes drifting along, and you whisk into the tunnel.

The tunnel: dark as the grave, cold, damp, and silent. How beautiful look earth and heaven again, as we emerge from the gloom! It might not be unprofitable, now and then, to send us mortals—the dissatisfied ones, at least, and that's a large proportion—into some tunnel of several days' journey. We'd perhaps grumble less, afterward, at God's handiwork.

Even rattling along after the steam-engine, people get a consciousness of the unrivalled beauties of Brooklyn's situation. We see the line of the Fifth Avenue, and the hills of Greenwood, and the swelling slopes that rise up from the shore, Gowanusward. Also the little cove that makes in by Freek's mill, and the meadows to the south of Penny Bridge, and the green knolls and the sedgy places below the aforesaid Fifth Avenue, and toward Bergen Hill.

But all the foregoing, (except the last paragraph) is only a flight of fancy—that took us back five or more years into the midst of the past. We put it down for the benefit of future readers (if we ever get them), who will not be aware that such a scene was of daily occurrence there at the South Ferry before the terminus was changed and the old tunnel filled up. Now the western extremity of the Long Island route is at Hunter's Point, just beyond Greenpoint—a handsome and thriving settlement that grows apace year after year, but does not exhibit the bustling and crowded aspect that for so many years marked the depot at South Ferry.

Still there is a horse railroad running from the latter place to East New York, where passengers proceed onward to

Jamaica, and so connect with the regular Long Island route. As we have had so much to say of the old depot of the just mentioned road, we may as well continue the theme by going down the line, and giving a brief mention of the places along it.

We will not stop any length of time at Bedford, except to tell our readers that the name it now goes by is the same name that was given it nearly a hundred years ago, by some English settlers there, and that it is one of the most ancient and charming sections of the consolidated City of Brooklyn. Some of the substantial old families of the city have their residences here, surrounded by ample grounds and choice shrubbery. Mr. Brevoort, the Lefferts, Mr. Betts, Mr. Redding, and others, are established here.

Proceeding to East New York, we find a flat and expanded tract, which is not only going to be a populous and wealthy settlement, but has already assumed that position. The writer of these various chronicles made the journey through this place, and down the whole length of Long Island, last autumn, and found East New York to have improved immensely from a few seasons since. From all accounts, it affords superior inducements to families who desire to be just out of the city, and yet within an hour's reach of it.

And so on to the Village of Jamaica, which is composed mostly of one long street, which is nothing else than the turnpike. It is lined closely by trees, which again have an inner lining of the same, sprinkled with shrubbery. As you enter the village you pass a pretty place some years since owned and occupied by Hackett the actor; more lately by Mr. Judd, a retired New Yorker. Then there is Gov. John A. King's residence unseeable from the road, through the impervious trees. We saw Mr. K., just returned from an agricultural fair, somewhere east. He holds his years well.

As you walk through the streets of Jamaica, every house seems either a store or a tavern. There are two newspapers, one by Mr. Brenton, otherwise "Dr. Franklin," a good soul; and the *Long Island Farmer*. Jamaica has a large, old established Academy for boys, "Union Hall," and also an Academy for Girls; the former having been in charge, in previous years, of Henry Onderdonk, an accomplished man of letters, whose interesting work on the "Revolutionary Incidents of Long Island" will hold a standard place in all our complete local libraries. The infinitude of Jamaica stores and public houses allows an inference which is the truth, viz.: that farmers, travellers, marketmen, and other passengers on the turnpike through the village give it all its trade and retail business. It has no manufactories, and has not been what is called a "growing place" for many years, and probably will not be.

We now come to an extensive and most interesting section of Long Island, and one which might have more reference to Brooklyn and its inhabitants than has hitherto been supposed. It is astonishing that immense quantities of good land lie yet untilled, within two hours' reach of this great city and New York. For after leaving Jamaica and Brushville, which is three miles east, we stretch out pretty soon upon "the Plains," that prairie-like and comparatively profitless expanse of land. The character of the country now becomes flat, and bare of trees; the houses are far from each other, and there is an uncomfortably naked and shrubless look about them. As the locomotive whisks us along, we see to a great distance on both sides, north and south—and see, mostly, large square fields, a great portion of which is devoted to pasturage.

The "Branch," or turning off place for Hempstead, is about eighteen miles from Brooklyn. A cluster of houses has been built up here, in the midst of the wide expanse, and a

tolerable degree of traffic is carried on; of course nearly all
derives its life-blood from the railroad—Hempstead, otherwise "Clamtown," otherwise "Old Blue," is some two miles
to the south; which two miles you pass over on a railway, in
cars drawn by horses that the crows, as they fly overhead,
must feel astonished at not having got some time before.
The village is rather a pleasant one, of perhaps 1400 inhabitants. It hath a Presbyterian tinge, of the deepest ceru-
lean; and in one of its graveyards is buried Henry Eckford,
the naval architect, who once held the office of chief con-
structor at the Brooklyn Navy Yard, and built that noble
piece of sea-craft, the ship of the line *Ohio*. Branching out
from Hempstead, in a southeasterly direction, is the fine
south turnpike, that leads along through (among other
places), Merrick, Babylon, Patchogue, Speonk, Good-
Ground, away east to the Hamptons.

For some miles east of "the Branch" there is little but a
mighty stretch of these uncultivated plains. True, there are
some patches inclosed, alongside of the railroad, here and
there. Around Hicksville, there is quite a group of these
settlings. Hicksville! that place of vanished greatness! O,
what a cutting up of lots and selling them off at high prices
there was here in "the time of the great speculation," years
ago! An immense city *was sure* to be that same Hicksville;
now its sovereign sway enfolds a large unoccupied tavern, a
few pig-pens, a very few scattered houses, and the aforesaid
little enclosures. But joking not, we shouldn't wonder to see
Hicksville gradually pick up and be a tidy little hamlet in the
course of a few years.

The great obstacle to improvement, all about here, is the
monopoly of most of this immense tract of plains, by the
Town of Hempstead, the people whereof will not sell, nor
divide it among themselves even, as was proposed a few
years ago. If they *would* consent to sell, the town treasury

would be prodigiously the gainer; and, cut up in strips, the land would be cultivated, adding to the looks of that region, to productiveness and human comfort, to the wealth of the Town of Hempstead, and consequently decreasing the rate of taxes. Some portions of the plains, belonging to the Town of Oysterbay, have been sold; and are taken up and settled on immediately.

Land monopoly shows one of its beauties most pointedly in this matter. We don't know, indeed, where one could go for a more glaring and unanswerable argument of its evils. Here is good land, capable of administering to the existence and happiness of thousands upon thousands of human beings, all lying unproductive, *within thirty miles of New York City,* because it is monopolized by one principal owner! We know the people save the right of pasturing their cattle, horses and sheep, on the plains—but that privilege, however widely used, does not develop one-twentieth of the resources of the land. Thousands of acres of it are covered with nothing but "kill-calf," and other thousands, where nothing grows, could be redeemed by two or three seasons' cultivation and manuring.

At Farmingdale, anciently known under the appellation of "Hardscrabble," you begin to come among the more popular specimens of humanity which good old Long Island produces. (Though we ought not to have overlooked the goodly Village of Jericho, two miles north of Hicksville— a Quaker place, with stiff old farmers, and the native spot of Elias Hicks.) Farmingdale rears its towers in the midst of "the brush," and is one of the numerous offspring of the railroad, deriving no considerable portion of its importance from the fact that the train stops here for the passengers to get pie, coffee and sandwiches.

We are now in the midst of the aforementioned "brush," a growth of pine and scrub-oak, mostly, though interspersed with birch, sumac, and other modest-sized trees. But at this time (late in the autumn) it is beautiful exceedingly! We can sit and gaze admiringly for miles and miles, at those colors that the chemistry of autumn has profusely dyed every leaf with. Deep and pale red, the green of the pines, the bright yellow of the hickory, are the prevailing hues, in numberless lovely combinations. We have often thought that those who make designs for carpets could get most excellent hints from these autumn garnishings. How pleasing and grateful would be a carpet pattern, richly covered with figures and colors, closely imitated from what one sees here— how much better than the tasteless, meaningless, and every way unartistical diagrams that we walk over, now, in the most fashionably carpeted parlors.

But our subject expands upon us, and we find it will be necessary to devote a special paper to some of the peculiarities of east Long Island. A very large portion of the inhabitants of Brooklyn are natives of the section, and will be able to test the truth of our remarks.

After leaving Farmingdale the railroad runs for about forty miles through a comparatively barren region, with stations every few miles, for the passengers for Babylon, Islip, Patchogue, etc., on the south side, and for Comac, Smithtown and divers other villages, toward the north. We arrive at Riverhead, which is the county seat of Suffolk, and quite a handsome village—pass on through Southold, and one or two other settlements, and whisk into Greenport, looking out upon Peconic Bay, of which more in our next.

XXI

TIES BETWEEN BROOKLYN AND THE EAST
END OF THE ISLAND

NOTES OF A VOYAGE OUT OF GREENPORT

THE START—THE COMPANY

GARDINER'S ISLAND—ITS HISTORY

Since we have roamed down the island, in the last two papers, and since there are such ties of connections between the eastern counties and this city of ours, we think it not at all amiss that our Brooklyniana sketches should extend themselves a little further on this occasion, and give some points of interest relating to the other extremity of Long Island; especially as there is no chance of their being chronicled by any body on the continental regions. We will therefore give some notes of an exploration journey, made by us last autumn, from Greenport out into the lands and waters thereunto adjoining. We suppose most of our readers are aware that Greenport is the terminus of the Long Island Railroad. It is a fine, half-rural, half-marine village, quite a summer and fall resort for sportsmen and fishermen. But to the account of my adventures (for it is now necessary to drop the editorial "we"), last fall, out of Greenport.

The black-fish were biting famously, and I stood at the end of the dock, quite proud of a big fellow I had just hauled up; and baited my hook again with "fiddlers," while the fish floundered at a great rate around my feet.

Just then a party of lively girls, conveyed by a clerical looking personage, and one or two younger fellows, came down the wharf, and betook themselves on board a taut and tidy sloop fastened there. Some large baskets also made their appearance. It was evidently a party off for a pleasure sail.

"Ease away your lines for a moment," said the young sailor who was working the sloop, to me and my companions, "till we shove along the pier."

I obeyed, and asked him where he was bound.

"To Montauk Point," he answered—adding, with sailor-like frankness, "Won't you go along?"

Upon the word, accoutred as I was, I plunged—the fish—into an old tin kettle, and gave them, with sixpence and my direction, to a young sea-dog who was in the predicament

of the celebrated Dicky Doubt, and jumped aboard, the
sailor good-naturedly holding fast to the wharf with a boat-
hook, and offering his shoulder for me to step on—though,
as he was about half my size, I thought it prudential to
decline.

As we pushed our sloop off from the pier's sheltering bul-
warks, the wind struck her, bellying out her sails and tilting
her down on one side in a decided and beautiful style, quite
to the water. I expected a few little screams, at least, from
the young ladies, but these east Long Island girls are terraqueous, like the men; long before our jaunt was over, I discovered that they could give me head-start and beat me all
hollow in matters connected with sailing.

It was a very pleasant and sensible party; the girls were
unaffected and knew a hawk from a hernshaw, and the
minister laughed and told stories and ate luncheons, just like
a common man, which is quite remarkable for a country
clergyman. I found him one of the pleasantest acquaintances
I had yet made on the island.

We sailed along at a stiff rate—told anecdotes and rid-
dles, and chatted and joked, and made merry. As for me, I
blessed my lucky stars; for merely to sail—to bend over and
look at the ripples as the prow divided the water—to lie on
my back and gaze by the half-hour at the passing clouds
overhead—merely *to breathe and live* in that sweet air and
clear sunlight—to hear the musical chatter of the girls, as
they pursued their own glee—was happiness enough for one
day. You may laugh at me, if you like, but there is an ecstatic
satisfaction in such *lazy philosophy,* such passive yielding up
of one's self to the pure emanations of nature, better than
the most exciting pleasures.

Rounding and leaving to the south "Hay-Beach" and
"Ram Head," two little capes of Shelter Island, we continued on our way rejoicing. The wind was stiff, while the

day was a warm one, which brought the temperature to just the right point.

Some miles ahead of us lay Gardiner's Island, like a big heart, with a bit of one of its edges sliced out. This fertile and "retired" little place, (the Indian name, *Monchonock*) contains about 3000 acres, mostly excellent land, and was originally purchased at the following price, according to the records:

One large black dog, one gun, a quantity (?) of powder and shot, *some rum,* and a few Dutch blankets.

This was in 1630; it is now worth seventy thousand dollars.

Gardiner's Island is historical in its association, to a more important pitch than is generally known, even on Long Island. It was the first English settlement ever made in the present limits of the State of New York. At first (1640, and forty years afterwards), it remained an independent little sovereignty of itself. Lion Gardiner, the purchaser and settler, seems to have been one of those massive old characters of the English commonwealth—belonging to the republican party of the early portion of the 17th century, with Hampden, Cromwell, and other hearts of oak. He was a civil engineer, and was sent over in "a small Norsey-Barque of 25 tons," to begin a fort at the mouth of the Connecticut River (Saybrook, I suppose, of course). He was an independent, God-worshipping man, and exercised great influence for good over both whites and Indians. The latter seem to have had unbounded confidence in him. Tradition relates that Wyandance, the great chief of east Long Island, loved and obeyed Mr. Gardiner in a remarkable manner, and, when he died, left to the honest Englishman the guardianship of his son, and desired him to be the advisor of his widow. By

Mr. Gardiner, also, the daughter of Wyandance, and thirteen other females who had been captured by Ninicraft, chief of a hostile tribe, and kept for a long time in durance, were restored to their parents and friends.

Imagination loves to trace (mine does, anyhow), the settlement and patriarchal happiness of this fine old English gentleman on his island there all by himself, with his large farm-house, his servants and family, his crops on a great scale, his sheep, horses, and cows. His wife was a Dutch woman—for thus it is written by his own hand in the old family Bible, which the Gardiners yet possess:

In the year of our Lord 1635, July the 10, came I, Lion Gardiner, and Mary my wife, from Woreden, a town in Holland, where my wife was born, being the daughter of one Derike Williamson, derocant, &c., &c.

Imagine the Arcadian simplicity and plenty of the situation, and of those times. Doubtless, among his work-people, Mr. Gardiner had Indians, both men and women. Imagine the picturesqueness of the groups, at night in the large hall, or the kitchen—the mighty fire, the supper, the dignity and yet good humor of the heads of the family, and the stalwart health of the brownfaced crowd around them. Imagine their simple pleasures, their interests, their occupations—how different from ours! And yet in all the deeper features of humanity—love, work, and death—they were the same.

We passed Gardiner's Island far to our left, and sped onward, hugging the shore of the peninsula of Montauk, and keeping a sharp lookout for shallow places, where we might risk the running on a sand bar. The long peninsula contains many thousands of acres, lying comparatively waste. And it makes one think better of humanity when he doth discover such a fact as I did in my travels, that this valuable tract of land is kept thus unseized and unsold by the Town of Easthampton, principally because the few remaining Indians hold in it a usufructuary interest, or right of enjoying and using it, though without any property in its soil.

The peninsula is nearly altogether used for pasturage, in shares, and is thus occupied by thousands of horses, sheep, etc., turned out to graze and grow fat. There is quite a peculiar race of fellows here, who live in huts by themselves, at large distances from each other, and act as horse-herds. You may be surprised, perhaps, to hear that occasionally these horses have a regular stampede, forming in solid bodies, charging along the open grounds at a tremendous rate, shaking the earth like thunder. The horse-herds have curious instruments, exactly on the principle of the toys vulgarly called "horse-fiddles"—and when these stampedes get under way, they rush out, and try to break the integrity of the enemy by whirling said instruments in a manner fast and furious.

Nigh one of the coves where our vessels passed, they showed me the cave of an old Indian hermit, who lived there. He was probably absent from home, as we saw nothing of him; though a young man, who formed one of our party, knew him very well, and on sporting expeditions had sometimes cooked a meal in his cave. From the young man's description, the old fellow must have been a pretty fair counterpart of Chingachgook, one of Cooper's Indian characters.

Montauk contains historical ground. It was the sacred burial place of the east Long Island Indians—their Mecca, and also their political centre. Wyandance lived there. The remains of the rude citadel occupied by this chieftain are yet to be seen, surrounded by innumerable Indian grave hollows. It was called *Duan-no-to-wouk.*

XXII

MONTAUK AND ITS PRESENT CONDITION

THE INDIANS NOW THERE

DESCRIPTION OF THE POINT

OUR PARTY IN GAY SPIRITS

Perhaps you would like to hear something about the present state of the Indian remnants on east Long Island. There are—so I am told—a few Indians more toward the western part of Easthampton, who live nearer to rational comfort and decorum; but the several specimens of men, women and children whom I saw were quite enough to take poetry out of one's aboriginal ideas. They are degraded, shiftless and intemperate—very much after the lowest class of blacks. They glean a sort of living out of their free range of the peninsula before mentioned, and by working for the farmers in harvest time, and selling baskets, mats and wooden ware, in making which they are very handy. The best thing connected with these poor devils is that they are not *very* thievish—perhaps, considering their poverty, less so than any known race of people. And Mr. Eels, of Brooklyn, who resided among the red men at the Northwest for many years, tells me that it is even to this day the same there. But I must keep on to Montauk Point, where we now arrive, and camp, our male and female party, myself and all.

Montauk Point! how few Americans there are who have not heard of thee—although there are equally few who have seen thee with their bodily eyes, or trodden on thy greensward. Most people possess an idea (if they think at all about the matter), that Montauk Point is a low stretch of land, poking its barren nose out toward the east, and hailing the sea-wearied mariner, as he approaches our republican shores, with a sort of dry and sterile countenance. Not so is the fact. To its very extreme verge, Montauk is fertile and verdant. The soil is rich, the grass is green and plentiful; the best patches of Indian corn and vegetables I saw last autumn are within gun shot of the salt waves of the Atlantic, being just five degrees east longitude from Washington, and the very extremest terra firma of the good State of New York.

Nor is the land low in situation. It binds the shore generally in bluffs and elevations. The point where the light-house stands—and it is the extreme point—is quite a high hill; it was called by the Indians *Wamponomon*—by modern folks Turtlehill. The light-house here is a very substantial one of an old-fashioned sort, built in 1795; the lights are two hundred feet above the level of the sea. Sheltered in a little vale, near by, is the dwelling of the keeper and his family, the only comfortable residence for many miles. It is a tolerably roomy cottage—a sort of public house; and some inveterate sportsmen and lovers of nature in her wild aspects come here during the summer and fall, and board awhile and have fun.

As every man was master of his time between our arrival and the period of dinner, I, with the rest of the party, took a good long ramble for several miles to and fro. To a mineralogist, I fancy Montauk Point must be a perpetual feast. Even to my unscientific eyes there were innumerable wonders and beauties all along the shore, and edges of the cliffs. There were earths of all colors, and stones of every conceivable shape, hue, and destiny, with shells, large boulders of a pure white substance, and layers of those smooth round pebbles called "milk-stones" by the country children. There were some of them tinged with pale green, blue or yellow—some streaked with various colors and so on.

We rambled up the hills to the top of the highest, we ran races down, we scampered along the shore, jumping from rock to rock we declaimed all the violent appeals and defiances we could remember, commencing with

"Celestial states, immortal powers, give ear!"

away on to the ending which announced that Richard had almost lost his wind by dint of calling Richmond to arms. I doubt whether these astonished echoes ever before vibrated with such terrible ado. Then we pranced forth again, like mad kine, we threw our hats in the air, aimed stones at the shrieking sea-gulls, mocked the wind, and imitated the cries of various animals in a style that beat nature all out!

We challenged each other to the most deadly combats— we tore various past passions into tatters—made love to the girls in the divine words of Shakespeare and other poets, whereat the said girls had the rudeness to laugh till the tears ran down their cheeks in great torrents. We indulged in some impromptu quadrills, of which the "chassez" took each participant couple so far away from the other that they were like never to get back. We hopped like crows; we pivoted like Indian dervishes; we went through the trial dance of *La Bayadère* with wonderful vigor; and some one of our party came nigh dislocating his neck through volunteering to turn somersaults like a circus fellow. Every body caught the contagion, and there was not a sensible behaved creature among us, to rebuke our mad antics by comparison.

XXIII

DIFFICULTY OF A DINNER

A NIGHT SCENE ON THE BAY

RETURN THE NEXT MORNING

A GOOD SPOT TO GO TO

Most appalling news met us on the return from this nice exercise! *Our master of the revels had utterly failed to negotiate a dinner for us at the cottage!*—Three several parties had been in advance of ours, that day, and had eaten up the last crumb in the house! Wasn't this enough to make Rome howl?

But it was no time to howl any more—we had already sharpened our appetites quite enough by that sort of sport. Something must be done, and quickly. A very fat, tender, plump-looking young woman was already trying to hide herself from the ravenous looks of two or three of the most alimentarily developed of our party, when we luckily spied a flock of well-grown chickens feeding near the cottage door. We had still lots of bread and butter aboard the sloop. Moreover, were there not the freshest and finest fish to be bought within stone-throw? And couldn't we get potatoes from that garden, and onions likewise? And what was better than *chowder?*

Our almost collapsed hearts now bounded up again like young colts. We proceeded in solid phalanx to the landlady —the Mrs. Light-house Keeper—and with an air which showed we were not going to stand on trifles, gave voice to our ultimatum. The landlady attempted to demur, but the major domo loudly proposed that if all else failed, we should eat the landlady herself; and this motion being passed by acclamation, the good woman gave in.

Six fat pullets had their heads off in as many minutes, and shortly afterwards we made a solemn procession down to the water, each man carrying a part of the provender, in its raw state. For we determined to cook our meal on board the sloop, and owe no thanks to those inhospitable shores. Our faithful major, at the head, carried a large sea-bass; next followed the young sailor with the six headless chickens, whose necks, (like Pompey's statue), all the while ran blood; next the fat girl with a splendid head of cabbage, behind whom marched the continuation of us, each furnished with something to make up the feast. Toward the rear came I, possessed of a stew-pan, purchased at a great price, and borne by me, I hope, with appropriate dignity.

All worked to a charm. Amid laughter, glee, and much good sport (though I and the fat girl cried bitterly, peeling onions), we cooked that dinner. And O ye Heavens, and O thou sun, that looked'st upon that dinner with a glow just as thou wast dipping thy red face below the western horizon —didn't we enjoy it? The very waters were as quiet as a stone floor, and we made a table by placing three boards on some barrels, and seats by other boards on half barrels. But the strangest part of all is that when we got through there were fragments enough to rival the miraculous remains of the feast of five loaves and two fishes. I shall remember that dinner to my dying day.

We pulled up stakes, and put for home. But we had over-stayed our time, and the tide too. Night came on. It was calm, clear and beautiful. The stars sparkled, and the delicate figure of the new moon moved down the west like a timid bride. I spread a huge bear-skin on the deck, and lay flat on it, and spoke not a word, but looked at the sky and listened to the talk around me. They told love stories, and ghost stories, and sang country ditties; but the night and the scene mellowed all, and it came to my ears through a sort of moral distillation; for I fear, under other circumstances, 'twould have appeared stale and flippant to me. But it did not then; indeed quite the contrary.

I made my bed in the furled sail, watching the stars as they twinkled, and falling asleep so. A stately and solemn night, that, to me, for I was awake much, and saw the count-less armies of heaven marching stilly in the space up there, marching stilly and slowly on, and others coming up out of the east to take their places. Not a sound, not an insect, interrupted the exquisite silence, nothing but the ripple of the water against the sides of the vessel.

Sunrise found us alive and stirring. We he-creatures departed for an island near by, on whose sedgy creeks there was the look of wild birds. Over the sand, here, we issued a second edition of the proceedings on the hills and shores of Montauk. But, owing to the absence of the terraqueous girls, we didn't have as good a time. After all, what a wretched place this earth would be without the petticoats!

A plentiful breakfast was ready when we returned; the Lord only knows whence came all the viands, for they appeared to rise, like Venus, from the froth of the sea. However, I asked no questions, but ate thankfully.

Up sails, then, and away!—a clear sky still overhead, and a dry, mild wind to carry us before it. I was astonished at the amount of vitality that resides in man, and woman too. One would have thought the exertions and outpourings we had performed within the last twenty hours should have left us cooled down a little. Angels bless you, sir! 'twas no such thing. Fast and loud rose the voices again, the clear upper notes of the girls, and laughter and singing. We knew we should soon be home—down amid the clouds and commonplaces—and we determined to make the most of it. And we *did*.

Ah, I despair of putting upon paper any true description of that condensed Babel. Our shouts transpierced the wounded air. Even the dullest of us seemed filled with mental quicksilver which rose higher and higher, until there seemed some chance of not enough being left in our heels to anchor us fast upon earth. Truly those were wonderful hours!

We hove in sight of the steeples and white paint of home, and soon after, the spirits we had served deserted us. (There was no brandy aboard, mind, and hadn't been.) We landed at the dock, and went up to the village, and felt the tameness of respectable society setting around us again. Doubtless it was all right; but as for me, I fancied I felt the mercury dwindling down, down, down into the very calves of my legs.

In conclusion, it must be confessed that the east end of Long Island, for a summer journey, affords better sport, greater economy, and a relief from the trammels of fashion, beyond any of the fashionable resorts or watering places, and is emphatically a good spot to go to, as many of our Brooklynites have long since discovered.